The Exit Is the Entrance

SERIES EDITOR
Nicole Walker

SERIES ADVISORY BOARD
Steve Fellner
Kiese Laymon
Lia Purpura
Paisley Rekdal
Wendy S. Walters
Elissa Washuta

The Exit Is the Entrance
Lydia Paar

The University of Georgia Press
ATHENS

Published by the University of Georgia Press
Athens, Georgia 30602
www.ugapress.org
© 2024 by Lydia Paar
All rights reserved
Designed by Erin Kirk
Set in Warnock Pro with Briston display
Printed and bound by Sheridan Books
The paper in this book meets the guidelines for
permanence and durability of the Committee on
Production Guidelines for Book Longevity of the
Council on Library Resources.

Most University of Georgia Press titles are
available from popular e-book vendors.

Printed in the United States of America
24 25 26 27 28 P 5 4 3 2 1

Library of Congress Cataloging-in-Publication Data

Names: Paar, Lydia, author.
Title: The exit is the entrance / Lydia Paar.
Description: Athens : The University of Georgia Press, [2024] | Series: Crux: the Georgia series in literary nonfiction | Includes bibliographical references.
Identifiers: LCCN 2024011471 (print) | LCCN 2024011472 (ebook) | ISBN 9780820367330 (paperback) | ISBN 9780820367347 (epub) | ISBN 9780820367354 (pdf)
Subjects: LCSH: Paar, Lydia—Childhood and youth. | Work—Psychological aspects. | LCGFT: Autobiographies. | Essays.
Classification: LCC PS3616.A227 E95 2024 (PRINT) | LCC PS3616.A227 (EBOOK) | DDC 814/.6 [B]—dc23/eng/20240426
LC record available at https://lccn.loc.gov/2024011471
LC ebook record available at https://lccn.loc.gov/2024011472

For Mum, and for Dana

The only way out is through.
—ROBERT FROST

Contents

Author's Note   ix
Prologue: Hol(e)y (I)   xi

An Escape Artist   1
Blockbuster   8
Drive (I)   16
The Cockroach Prayer   20
Formula   44
Hol(e)y (II)   56
Pulse   66
Drive (II)   78
Erasure   80
Drive (III)   100
Magnet Man   103
Passage   114
Osmosis   127
Murder City   175
Hope for Sale   184

Epilogue: Drive (IV)   210

Acknowledgments   213
About the Author   215

Author's Note

The word "essay," in addition to describing the short form of non-fiction writing contained here, has a double meaning as a verb: to try. And that's what I'm up to in this book: trying to make sense of some things. It should be acknowledged that my perception is as subjective as anyone else's, though I've tried to reconstruct and depict the events mentioned fairly and in good faith. It should also be noted that I've changed some names to direct attention toward the experience and understanding of such events, and away from any resonating indictment of specific individuals. I thank you for sharing this goal of seeking understanding, if you want to share it. Either way, I thank you for reading.

Prologue   Hol(e)y (I)

"I'm going to escah-pay."

You say it like the Greek word "agape," a childlike mispronunciation from the film *Finding Nemo* that you like because the rhyme reminds you: departing from things that don't work can offer hope for deeper unity. And if there's no exit, you can make one. In the army, to make a hole (H), one parts a little sea of soldiers like a military Moses to make a channel through which goods or other people may move quickly under duress. Unity becomes inherent again; it just happens in a new direction now, across connections that had become, from other angles, barriers, requiring breaking.

Have you ever noticed that the homonyms "whole" and "hole" are also, at first glance, antonyms, bound up together in a sideways kind of logic? To make a hole (with an H), one skewers a (W) whole, seemingly destroying unity, but then bringing it back in new shapes: Christ's lanced ribs, and the stigmatic hands of his holiest followers, who provided paths for people to clearly see cruelty, then its alternatives. An escape hatch from having to damage each other, historically, continuously. The soft but demanding suction pulls you through something known and painful and out into something new, and more hopeful.

Once, you found yourself on a ferry in New York, suspended in the seeming-calm sheet of East River between Staten Island where you lived and Wall Street where you worked. You sat at the back of the ferry and pretended it was a pleasure cruise instead of a ride to work. You sat at the back because Jacques, your roommate ex-CIA foreign correspondent, told you that if anybody bombed the ferry, they'd secure the explosive to the front; when the hole was blown out, the engine would continue to drive the vessel forward down into the deep. Passengers who'd just been leaning on that front rail, pointing forward toward the future, would be sucked into history, while those lingering at the back, like you, could jump away.

You told this, Jacques's advice, to your brother when he moved to New York, but he seemed in a funk and didn't much care. Depression, your sometimes-depression-prone dad told you, runs in the family. It's a selfish disease, he said, like a black hole to pull you inside yourself and then inside out. What's at the center of yourself, once you get there? No one really knows.

What's at the center of a black hole? People still guess at that too. Your best friend from middle school studies physics. You seem to recall her mentioning that matter sucked into a black hole might compact and crush, almost like reverse growth. Before she finished her PhD, you'd appeared at her apartment, AWOL from the army. She gave you shelter for a few days before you caught a bus home. You lost track of her for a decade after that, the same in which two of your good friends died by knife or by bullet hole. When you found her again, her brother had shot himself.

You've somehow always escah-payed from places that risked an irreparable hole, or too many holes, to yourself. Most of your friends and family, including your brother, are still okay too. Your brother, in fact, has moved to Florida, where the sun shines bright and holes move horizontally and somehow vertically both, filled with salty rain sucked up from the sea. You hope that if your brother is ever caught up in one, he's funneled upward all the way to the sky, so he can see for miles—see that unity, after all, is still inherent. Then he will not be frightened, or sad.

You hope the same for everyone, metaphorically.

Escah-pay.
Agape.
Make a (W)Hole.

The Exit Is the Entrance

An Escape Artist

It starts here: at the window in the ten-by-five wood-paneled room in the attic. I stare out the window, through the bars my grandma had installed, not to keep people out, though this Portland neighborhood has had robberies, but to keep me in. We've moved here, my mother and brother and I, to live with our grandparents since our mom and dad divorced and we came back from Kentucky. We occupy the attic, which is large for an attic, though we still have to duck down in the corners. My brother, I call Bobey (long o—like Bohb, with an eeeee on the end), after a character in a play I once wrote as a kid. I don't know why this nickname stuck.

Bobey is better at sneaking out than me. "I just walk through the house," he says. But I'm afraid of being noticed by Gramma, so I climb out my window.

If you lean carefully on the release bar latch, you can spring the window bars without too much noise. Then you can slide the old single-paned window wide open, hoist yourself around, and lower yourself, legs first, slowly down until your toes touch the back staircase railing. There's a second, between pushing yourself off the windowsill and when your foot reaches the railing, where you're suspended by nothing: everything could go wrong. And yet, usually it doesn't, except the time you landed on the railing a little hard, and it broke. That's how you got the bars.

Once you're down, you can sneak through the backyard and the driveway and up 52nd Avenue to Powell, where you can meet your friend Brad, who has ridden from his wealthy neighborhood on a bike, and walk back together to his neighborhood: share a pair of headphones with a Discman playing nineties alt-rock, stop at Plaid Pantry for candy, sneak down into the lush and rolling Eastmoreland golf course and light the trash barrel in the bathroom on fire. You can tag the walls with personalized graffiti you both find pretty. Maybe make out, or more. Take a nap someplace. As the sun comes up, walk back home and tell your mom you were out for an early walk.

Time and space spread wide.

Eventually the sneaking out becomes harder. Brad's parents keep a closer eye on him. The boy, not Brad, who is officially your boyfriend but who feels more like a friend, finds out about all this too, and we all know what happens to girls who stray. A social snubbing at school can have an unintended bonus, though: new focus.

Maybe, if I have a job, I think to myself, I'll get to buy a car, and then some freedom. I could drive to the beach. Or at least do my homework at a coffee shop. But who will hire a fourteen-year-old?

Subway will, says my school friend Sarah.

I interview with Michele, who smokes a cigarette while reading my handwritten application. She's irreverent, and homely, and nice, and she hires me on the spot.

Now we are all on shift together, me, Sarah, and her two public-school pals who become my pals too, our polo shirts slightly stained, our visors straight. "Sandwich Artist" is what the visor says across the front. But mine should say "Escape Artist," for this new job is how I will escape being broke.

As the line wraps around the deli's center seating, we form a fireman's brigade for sandwiches: Sarah slices bread, Becky slaps down meat and cheese, Julie counts two tomato slices, four pickles, and six olives per six-inch (double for a footlong). I stuff in the lettuce, squirt sauces, wrap and bag the sub, then give it to the cashier, usually a manager.

In between rushes we'll restock.

"Oops!" I cringe, arriving at the back prep counter in the aftermath of the last mid-lunch rush. The meat's been left out, and now it's sweating.

Simon, my manager, motions me toward him at the walk-in.

"Here."

And hands me a green pepper, hollowed out to make a makeshift pipe. Because I'm fourteen, I've not learned yet that getting stoned and trying to do anything other than eat is futile. So it takes me longer, after I leave the frost of the giant fluorescent-lit fridge, to rewrap my meat, mop the floor.

As I glob mayonnaise into a dinged metal bowl of partially thawed faux-crab mix, a wayward nosy customer spies me and asks, "Is there dolphin meat in there?"

"Nope," I retort. The tender pink crab is clearly pictured on the menu board above: no dolphin.

But then I realize: Who knows what gets into hasty fishing nets along the way? Who will dare to care? Not us, for $5.50 an hour. That $5.50 will barely buy my pack of Camels, which I will talk my mom's biker boyfriend into purchasing post-work, before it occurs to him to hock our family's jewelry and TV for his eventual backslide into drugs.

I go on to squish the fish and mayo together until it looks blended, then plop it all in a big plastic tub. I drop the tub into the front food line and step outside through the side door to see the sun setting softly over the adjacent shopping-center parking lot.

Then I see them: my well-moneyed friends, the ones from Central Catholic, from Eastmoreland: the ones who don't work. They find it fun that I work at Subway, though, because I get one free sandwich per shift, and they can try to relieve me of mine. Sometimes I give in, making their orders when none of the other bosses is around. But I like my own sandwiches: I'm hungry in general, and with a lightning metabolism. ("Anorexia," they whisper, but no.) I crave BLTs, but also a sense of adventure alongside my chicken bacon ranches, meatball marinaras, and mirages of adulthood soon to come and release me from my boring daily toils here in teenagehood. I consume my sandwiches and my visions, then smoke my cigarettes, a new habit I've adopted after Boss Michele, and it will be years before I come to understand I'm the only worker who takes the legally allotted fifteen-minute breaks (one per four hours) because I smoke, and if I don't, I get bitchy.

So anyway, I step outside to smoke and talk with the Eastmoreland kids. They're having dinner soon, they tell me, then maybe they'll try to shoulder-tap some beer. I should join them.
    Though sometimes annoying, these particular kids can be fun, in a risky kind of way. The last time we all hung out—it was six or seven of us—we walked to the Reed College campus, empty in spring break, to an old student rec hall, and pushed each other over the wooden balcony there out of shopping carts, falling fifteen feet or so onto a stack of piled-up old couch cushions.

I agree to join them. Across the parking lot at Wong's Garden, after my shift, the appetizers arrive. The small group of us are so obnoxious (mainly the boys) that a man at the next table over, middle-aged and on a date with a shy-seeming woman in coral lipstick and a floral dress, asks us twice to quiet down: we're rude with our cursing. Backtalk ensues. I don't recall who told him to fuck off first, but I have my guess: the richest boy from Eastmoreland. I think it was the poor white trash boy of the group—pal by proxy—who first invited him out to the parking lot to clear it all up. I don't recall who threw the first punch, man or boy, but what happened next etches irrevocably into my mind: my so-called "friends" circling the older man, then a flurry of punches until he falls down.

I yell for them to stop, but they're well past that.

When I storm off crying, the man's sandy blond head and work boots curl together like a shrimp as he tries to fend off their feet, coming in straight to his ribs.

I'm sure there is something more I should have done, but that's what I did. On the Subway steps again, lighting a shaky cigarette, I take out my flip phone to dial 9-1-1 on my friends. But then Vick, the other girl in the group, comes and asks why I left. The ruckus is over now. The overworked restaurant owner broke it up.

I try to explain how disgusted I am, how upset. I'm gulping for air as I gesture.

Well, she says, it's over now anyway: the boys got kicked out, and they're going to one of their houses to hang. The richest boy lives the closest, the boy I remember baiting the man.

"Are you coming?"

"Are you kidding?"

I suck my smoke down madly as she shrugs and walks back to join them.

I don't know this then, but in the future, more than once again, I'll find myself wondering how people I know, people I'm close to, can tolerate cruelty in certain unexpected circumstances. The realization will disturb me each time it happens, and each time it happens, I will lose a little faith in human goodness.

I'm still mad as I stub out my cigarette.

After I realize I must make new friends, I spend more time at work the next few weeks. I pick up as many shifts as I'm allowed and go straight to work after school. I begin to date Simon, the manager. He's nineteen and a gentleman. I'm now fifteen, but since we don't fuck, we're legal.

One night he agrees to drop me off at home after work and save my mom a trip. He's tallying digits from the printout register tape.

While he writes numerical notes into his manager's log, and while I'm spraying down the dining room with bleach dilution, I spy a long, thick manila envelope stuck tight between booth and white wall.

From it I extract two X-rays, revealing two peanutty hemispheres of human brain.

I hold the slides up to the light, let my eyes wander around in the crinkles till they fixate on a single spot, round and opaque.

Squashed beneath the X-rays is a loose page of notebook paper, folded in an awkward little square.

I fish it out, and upon unfolding, blue handwriting scrawls sideways, asking, almost excitedly and certainly erratically, if the new tumor (the spot?), the one the author has just learned has blossomed in their brain, could be a blessing.

Doctors don't know if it's operable, the author says, but tumors can press down on new nerves, reroute blood flow, bestow almost alien abilities like telepathy.

Maybe, the author wonders, a new connection could be forged, an open channel to the divine, even though, or perhaps because, death is suddenly more imminent: an architecture of hope not based in survival but in surrender.

I flap the folder shut. As I tuck it under my arm, Simon approaches with my coat and lifts an eyebrow.

"What's that?"

I tell him it's attempted redemption.

On the way home, I think about the episode from weeks earlier at Wong's Garden. At nineteen, Simon's only three years older than those dumb Eastmoreland kids. As his 1970s gold Camaro grumbles up to Gramma's, I think to myself how Simon's really, despite his youth, kind of middle-aged: polite, honest, steady, and with a work ethic as indefatigable as that of his blue-collar family back East. He has the same Carhartt jacket as the man I saw beaten. Simon's not a coward, like me. He would have said something, stopped those spoiled boys from kicking a downed man on his date, on his date after a workday long enough that he didn't change out his work jacket.

"Why are you keeping this?" Simon asks, handing me the X-ray envelope, and I tell him it's "because someday the owner might return for his redemption."

But maybe it's because I'm seeking some too.

I still smell his cologne, comforting, as I ascend the stairs to my room. My family is sleeping, and the only thing I hear is myself, creaking up each carpet-covered, worn-wood step. The upstairs, the attic, is musty. I'll go kiss my mom in a moment. But first, a moment to myself.

As I slide my window open to bring in the air, I see the street-lit high school parking lot next door, fuzzy in the fog. Some kids are yelling over the revving of truck engines, trunks thudding with bass. Like the shrimp from Wong's Garden, we teens can form such large schools during spawning. Tender under skins, thinner than transparent shells, our greatest human growth spurt lasts about as long as the longest Caridean lifespan.

Then what?

Who are we to be?

I light my cigarette, which has nothing to do with survival and everything to do with hope.

I curl my fingers around it in the semblance of the beat-up Carhartt man.

Blockbuster

1999: year of Y2K fever.
Millennial fear.
The year of living in the moment in your fear: *The Blair Witch Project*, running us around a semidark campsite, first-person shooter style and shaky on a handheld cam, until we leaned over seasick in theaters.

The cults have gone crazy, but I'm just happy to be graduating from high school. I'm not exactly sure what I will do after high school, but it's got to be better than what I currently do: smoke cigarettes for breakfast en route to morning Spanish class; read, listen vaguely, and take tests all day; then drive my 1983 hatchback home to write essays, or up 39th Street to gritty Powell Boulevard, to the giant, warehouse-like square of a Blockbuster movie store there. If I'm there for a night of work, rather than a night of movie-renting pleasure, I slip my uniform collared shirt over my tank top in the bright-white-plastic-tabled, fluorescent-lit break room. Pin on my nametag. Tuck my hair back with some bobby pins, and prepare to smile.

At the register station I may find myself scanning bar codes and upselling our membership plan. But if I'm lucky, I get to work at the reshelving station instead and spend more time browsing the massive selection of stories we peddle, sometimes selling, more often renting them, to people of all ages, races, and economic walks of life. In this particular neighborhood, close to my house, we serve many Eastside blue-collar customers, and also a lot of adolescents, a life-path portrayal I seek in new releases but find more commonly scattered through shelves of earlier films: 1999 is a year of romancing riches. When I work late, though, and the rush of fast headlights from Powell bathes me through the storefront's tall windows, I feel lucky: I may be among a demographic unromanced by current Hollywood directors, but I'm still pretty safe, behind glass, here in Blockbuster fantasyland. I could, with a few unfortunate shifts in circumstance, end up in something more like *My Own Private Idaho* (a 1991 flick from the cult classic shelf) and have to do far harder "customer service" work.

About a year back, I was trained by Crystal, a curly-haired twentysomething manager with glitter nail polish and a rare good-lipstick-and-glasses combo, to scan my way through stacks of waiting movies, rewind them in one of four open-jawed rewinding machines, and walk long circles around the store to reshelve them.

There's a method to it: Pile up a stack, the length of your arms, which fits snugly between your hands and your chin. Make sure it's piled up mostly alphabetically, as the new releases go A–Z except for real blockbusters, which sometimes take up a whole section and so jog the expected order. Then leave the associates-only area to mosey around the thinly carpeted center of the store and encircling wall racks, unless, of course, it's busy, in which case speed quickly to avoid customer questions while carrying the awkward VHS and DVD load. Standing before the correct empty plastic film case, you can tip yourself back to balance your stack of movies against your chest and right arm simultaneously, then use the index finger of your left hand to tip the plastic case with its colorful front, which lives always on the rack, forward. Then simply slide the video you've picked off the top of your stack behind it, also with your left hand. Rebalance and repeat.

Some of the films are reflective, like I hope to be someday about my future interesting life, but in a better way than, say, *American Beauty*, whose protagonist, now dead, looks back at his life but finds it as bitter as it has been sweet.

In the meantime, my seventeen-year-old self finds herself stuck in seventeen-year old reality: *American Pie*. Or *Varsity Blues*, which I never watch because I hate sports.

I seek *Sleepy Hollow*. *The Sixth Sense*. *The Matrix*.

Films of awakening, revelation. *The Green Mile*.

Art-house films that meander through stories slowly, to let the audience make more of the meaning, like those I went to see with The Boy I Am Sweet On: the boy with lean arms and finely arched eyebrows from the upper-crust family (at least by Portland standards) whose dad was a doctor.

Whose pool party I attended mildly drunk because I was afraid of this unfamiliarity.

Who I tipsily left a tiny love note for on my way back, lost, from the bathroom, passing, only by chance, his open bedroom door.

In the cinema, an old Portland building with balcony seating, he and I watched *Beau Travail*, a spectacular vision of French soldiers stationed in Djibouti, full of hard training, high-heat endurance, a jealous officer who leaves a soldier he both loves and hates to die alone in the desert.

1999: the year of frustrated affection: again, *American Beauty*. And loving the things you hate. Or loving to hate: *Fight Club*.

Crystal, my boss, quit or was fired not long after hiring me. She mentioned a boyfriend on meth. In line with trending corporate oversight, I get three new bosses: a boom of middle management. But my new bosses are nice. They are flexible about my schedule. I can ask for days off in advance—for parties, or pre-test evenings—and actually get them. I also already get five free rentals per week (to help us better talk with customers), but sometimes the nice bosses let me sneak a couple more.

It's a year of kind strangers, unlikely endings: *Pretty Woman*.

A year, too, of waiting ambition: *The Talented Mr. Ripley*.

Which sometimes doesn't work out, thinking you can beat your predetermined place in the world with love and just a dash of smart thinking.

Maybe I never see *Pretty Woman* because I already believe these ideas.

Or because I already don't.

The Boy I Am Sweet On recommends *The Talented Mr. Ripley* to me, and after renting it, I don't know why. Is it beautiful Gwynyth Paltrow, made up as girlfriend Maeve? Is it Italy, sun-drenched and seaside?

I wonder, eventually, if it's because he knew how much work it really took to be upper crust: quiet codes, unspoken rules.

At his house (a small mansion? I think so) I feel like a character from *Being John Malkovich*, dropped suddenly, and only momentarily, into a strange and rule-bent world, where people's idiosyncrasies are simply accepted, not covered up under uniforms.

His soft-spoken mother kneels oddly next to his father, she sewing on the floor and he sitting in his chair while we all watch TV.

Perhaps she's as uncomfortable with me there as I am, telling The Boy later, privately, I'd stayed too late.

Meanwhile, me, trying not to cause trouble: just lost again on the way to find the bathroom, glancing out a window and longing to swim down in the bright blue backyard pool below.

Evenings at Blockbuster, I buy candy with my discount for my dinner. I like the cookie dough balls coated in chocolate, or their sister version, in fudge. Sometimes I will supplement with popcorn. I look forward to the day I will work at a place with real meals again. Or even a better job, but I don't have an imagination about what that might be: what it is like to be "in business," a path many classmates are tracing. One coworker of mine wants to be a cop. Another, a lawyer. But he doubts he'll ever get there: too pricey.

In the time of middle management, of in-betweens, I keep waiting for good music to resurge, reenergized from the sixties, seventies, eighties, early nineties, with tangled ballads and wild, wistful disco beats: dance halls, dirges, and unfettered urges.

But everything on the radio, tucked in these movie soundtracks, seems derivative. All the rock bands are bitching about high school, just like I do. The teen flicks are old stories, with tired morals, recycled and dressed up in Doc Martens: *She's All That* (*Pygmalion*). *Ten Things I Hate About You* (*The Taming of the Shrew*). *Cruel Intentions* (*Les Liaisons Dangereuses*). Even *Beau Travail* was ripped off from *Billy Budd*.

One day, I ask The Boy I'm Sweet On to pull over on the way to my house so I can smoke a cigarette. I can't smoke in his parents' Jaguar, so I step outside, expecting him to stand with me and chat. But he waits in the car. I decide that *He's Just Not That Into Me* [*sic*] a decade before the similarly named film comes out, and I go about my in-between: working late on weeknights, partying with hooligans, lighting cigarettes after every new *A* that I log on my report card, and sleeping with boys I secretly wish were The Boy I Am Still Sweet On, but who are not. The Boy I Am Sweet On applies to Columbia. I tell him New York sounds awfully big. I think maybe I am not big enough for it, or for him.

Another day, I'm hanging out with some hooligans at a new pal's house, a public school kid who dropped out. His mom works all day. Her bed is covered in clothes. The new friend plays video games all day. His basement is full of shit. The group of us sit in the basement, amidst a three-foot pile of fast-food bags, candy wrappers, dirty socks, hollow beer cans.

All our other friends have trickled away to the warm air outside while we continue to sit next to each other in the basement, and he eventually, casually, moves his elbow over onto my thigh.

His hands still hold the game controller.

His elbow on my thigh feels good.

The kiss is fun enough. But then I want to go.

And he begs.

"You led me on," he says.

It's ancient risk, reignited: *Star Wars* (*The Phantom Menace*). *The Mummy*.

It's self-blinding: *Eyes Wide Shut*.

I tell myself, upstairs in his bedroom, on his dirty, unmade mattress, that I've brought this on myself: I didn't demur enough, and my "no" caved into "okay." And control, however haphazardly employed, sounds better to me than the other thing this feels like (*Rape*, a minor film that year; it never hit the New Releases rack).

. . . Which it's technically not, because somehow I agreed. It doesn't hurt *that* bad, as I wince and try not to cry. I haven't seen much porn yet, so I don't know that women sounding pained during sex is a trope.

Afterward I go home, take a bath. Sit sadly in lukewarm water, sleep early.

I don't do anything different for a week: just work and study. As in *The Virgin Suicides*, it's likely that no one else thinks anything much is even wrong, but I'm mad, and mostly at myself.

I don't call The Boy I Am Sweet On anymore, but one too-quiet evening The Boy I Slept With By Mistake calls me.

I find that despite my initial aversion, it feels relieving to get the call.

Perhaps it's just nice to get *a* call.

When I see myself in *The Mirror*, I doubt my suspicion and self-righteousness: who am I to judge someone's lack of education, his dirty home?

Maybe no one's told him he has a hurtful initial approach to "dating."

Maybe I should.

I'm certainly not the first teen for whom boredom and sadness birth the will to make "projects" of unlikely lovers: the Pygmalion-paradigmatic *She's All That* still sells out most weekends.

So, in the summer of 1999, I try to grow empathy, however naïve: like Woody for Buzz Lightyear in *Toy Story 2*. I ride passenger in The Accidental Boyfriend's Chevy Nova, shoulder-tap beer from old homeless guys with him, have more painful sex on the sheetless mattress, and watch his friends play video games in his garbage-filled basement. He and I have a private dinner date only once that I can recall, but my generally hopeful worldview gleaned from the movies—that one can make a positive difference in the condition of one's life—can remain, at least, more or less intact.

When he tells me one day, casually sitting on his porch, that he's bored and wants to break up, I feel duped.

When he brings his new girlfriend to Blockbuster for a movie the following week, my nice boss lets me hide from them in the break room.

And when I hear rumors that he's developed a stomach disease, I smile, breaking the Polite Portlander script. I feel vengeful, like Stephen King's *Carrie*, conveniently remastered in *The Rage: Carrie 2*, for 1999's newly prom-aged audience.

I bide my remaining time in adolescence anxiously, *Runaway Bride* style, waiting to bolt from all this business into my new future.

When I do bolt, after high school and from Blockbuster, the result is spectacularly disastrous: there are fireworks in my forthcoming failures.

Some would-be box-office flops of mine:

Quitting College Blues (I, II, and III)
Ten Things I Hate About Office Jobs
The Credit-Debt's-a-Bitch Project
My Own Private Basic Training Bunk Bed
(and its sequel: *A.W.O.L.*)

I can puncture the foreshadowing for you: an arguably more or less dramatic *Girl, Interrupted*, I will make many wrong moves and lose my direction for some good few years more (though, thankfully, I won't land in a psych ward).

Eventually, after a while, things will straighten out. My personal narrative will rise and arc. I just know it: I'll find my way to great climaxes, some lovely and restful denouements.

The cinematography, at moments, will be scenic.

But I suspect it will take time: unwinding like my favorite mystery show, *The X-Files*, to get to the goodness and illumination over years, rather than the standard two-hour allotment of most modern movies.

Sometime, though, between my teens and late twenties, Blockbuster quietly shuts up shop. From what I know, only one store remains now, also in Oregon but in a smaller, more out-of-the-way town than Portland. You can finally buy all those movies they liquidated for cheap now, online, to keep and watch again and again. But conveniently, most Americans don't even have to: for a cheaper monthly membership than those I sold in high school, we can mainline all the imagined realities we want, unlimited, straight into our living rooms through one of many available streaming services. A current favorite, also from 1999: *Law and Order, Special Victims Unit*, whose universal themes of need, penetration, and power are still relevant today and keep them filming fresh episodes even now.

Drive (I)

When I was a teenager, I wished to be a trucker. I should say, rather, the profession was in my top-ten list of future plans.
 I was drawn to open roads.
 Delighted at the thought of a distant boss, I ached for new lands.
 Airbrakes excited.

But I determined, instead, to stay in school a bit longer. I'd been advised to take pre-calc instead of personal finance, so I didn't understand student debt, plus my college-prep high school had a habit of reading aloud acceptance lists and scholarships at graduating senior ceremonies: no pressure.
 There was a path prescribed, and we were all supposed to take it. So my mom helped me mail some applications: one to a nearby state school and one for a fancy private college, which happened, after all, to offer loans.
 They took me in, and we took a bus down to the fancy one: just Mum and I are our luggage, over one paltry state line.

Northern California had mountains like heaven, and we carved wide around them on giant Western roads. Some sections stretched vast, like where the bus broke down and we deboarded: six lanes deep of fast traffic.
 Smog seethed at the teeth.

Mum was suffering from diverticulitis, where weaker portions of the intestinal wall pooch out into little pouches under pressure, catching food particulate, inflaming the imperfect maze of the gut, and causing pain.

She had turned near-to-green as we'd groaned up the massive green hills, then, after the bus emptied out, a ghostly pale by the street side.

"I think you'll like it here." She smiled weakly. Patted my hand. I gazed out at everything unfamiliar.

"At least it has a view," I said.

A new bus arrived from the smog and sank us like an airplane through just-orange-tinged cloud tops into shimmering, filthy Los Angeles.

Mum cried, leaving me at the fancy college to fly home.

I sat amidst manicured lawns and string quartet dinner shows and my Self succumbed to sorrow. What if Mum died while I was here, sitting in this manicured grass? Or just slogged through her sickness without me? I didn't belong here anyway: my working class was showing. I couldn't feel my purpose, or my future, pulsing between well-paved roads, pools, and pedi paths.

I didn't take a bus when I backtracked, a mere three months later.

But I could still use a credit card to skip the hard road home: an Airbus this time, passing 900 miles over both car and cloud northbound in the middle of the night.

One year later I'd run away again, not from college, or from home, but from basic.

This time my softness was showing: I'd acquired four broken bones between all the army exercises, and despite my now uselessness at drills, they weren't going to let me go.

So I snuck away. I'll tell you how, soon.

Afterward, I couldn't take a plane: too trackable. But on buses then, you didn't have to have ID.

So I cruised discreetly west from South Carolina, a vaguely Oregon Trail rendition, on another grumbling Greyhound.
Columbia. Atlanta. Louisville.
St. Louis in the thick black of night: no Gateway Arch visible as we barreled through, eyes shuttered.
Kansas City, then Lawrence as the light returned. A long stretch of another day to Denver.
By the next morning in Wyoming, we breakfasted. Cheyenne had homestyle hash browns, undercooked. Thick, like my ankles, swollen from immobility.

At one point the bus was tagged by a little commuter car, and a cop car arrived, red lights illuminating the back bathroom I thought I'd hide in if the police, for some reason, decided to board. But they didn't—they had better things to do—so we continued onward, dipping into the desert, where long tongues of natural gas flame leapt out bright against the blue.

I was trying to sleep as the bus sleeked forward some more, a Salt Lake-bound soaring tuna can.
"Where ya headed?" asked the gentleman to my left, recently arrived, waking me and breaking my reverie.
I've been raised to respect my elders, and since he was wrinkled and bald, I told him: Oregon, westmost West.
"Wow!" His eyebrows lifted. "Long haul!"
He himself hadn't far to go: just had to catch up with his carnival.
"That's your job?" I asked, eyes widening now.
And he replied, "Carny for life!"
He'd run away, at fourteen, he said, to join.
Found freedom.

He told me stories of wandering characters I can't now remember, performers and others he'd met along the way on road trips just like this. But I remember his special skill-sharing clearly:
"Wanna know how to get drunk on a bus?"

Pulled from his backpack: a netted bag of oranges.

"You can't bring cans on—they'll kick you off—but if you take a syringe—"

I didn't ask him why he'd have one handy.

He mimed pulling up a plunger, peeking a needle in through the netting. "—and inject each orange with the vodka. Voila! The driver thinks you're snacking."

He peeled one of the fruits and offered me a slice.

Then he flapped out a napkin and folded it, fashioned a rose.

"Here," and gave it to me.

"I wish you all the luck getting home."

The Cockroach Prayer

As I recall, the weather was quite nice: breezy, with steady sunlight, a few dappled clouds. I was stuck inside, looking out a tinted window, squirming in my seat, which was not allowed.

Shit, I thought, I'm going to miss pictures. Another anonymous corporal I don't remember well was taking my blood because I couldn't recall whether mine was A or AB, and they didn't want to impress the wrong one into my dog tags. As my drill sergeant had barked, "That would be a serious fuck-up, Private." He's right, I thought. What a silly way to go: death by transfusion.

I held the tags up to the sunlight when they passed them out later in the afternoon. Everyone got two: one they would secure somehow with your body, tucked discreetly in your mouth if you still had a mouth, and the other they would send back to your unit commanders, so they could write a tidy letter to your family. This was in the case that you happened to die in combat, which none of us would have to worry about, our recruiters said: "Your unit won't see combat this decade."

I turned to Webster, my "battle buddy," always at my side.

"Hey, we're in the army," I said. "Or at least, we're going to be reservists."

"Yeah, it's official," she replied, even though it had really been official the day we both folded up our own glasses (mine leopard print, hers teal) and traded them out for army glasses. Army glasses made us look exactly alike, which was always the point; we became two fine-haired, sunburnt blondes with half our faces enveloped by thick brown Coke-bottle lenses. We were allowed to take our glasses off for the picture, Webster told me that evening, as we sat on our bunks swinging our dog tags around, and I was irritated that I'd missed my opportunity to record my experience there permanently. Who would believe, without such proof, that I, the wannabe liberal-arts major, would have gone to basic training? I almost wouldn't believe it myself.

Growing up, I had many identities. As a toddler, I was the hot-headed "prickly cactus" who kicked her infant brother—who had plugged sinuses and a permanently open, drool-emitting mouth—off a yellow-upholstered rocking chair for attempting to climb up and sit with her. As a four-year-old, I was an enterprising salesperson who marched bags of acorns around the neighborhood in a red Radio Flyer wagon to sell as "squirrel food" to people who mostly wished the squirrels dead. As a middle schooler, a glutton for every subject except math, a tomboy who kicked the boys in the balls when they made fun of her girlfriends. As a high schooler, a refined kind of depressed poet who liked to sneak out at night. By age nineteen, I had come to self-identify as a college dropout office worker. I held small children still while the nurses at my allergy research clinic drew their blood. This GI Bill, however, could pay my tuition at the pricey second private school I'd been accepted to, Reed College, where they had dormitories that looked like medieval castles and a school seal like a coat of arms from ancient Europe. Since I would only be on reserve, I could take classes like normal, go to a well-paid weekend/monthly training that would substitute for daily waitressing, and have free standby flights on military aircraft all over the world.

My parents, who'd met in the army, thought the idea was a little quirky but just might work. They'd met translating Russian for the army over in Germany, after all, and the GI Bill had been the purchasing power for our first house. My grandpas had both been in World War II and Korea: commanding officers. Bobey thought I was nuts. My friends were worried, but they nonetheless threw me a birthday party seven days before I took a plane from Portland to the south, then a rickety old bus that pulled up and dumped me squarely into the sticky heat of Fort Jackson, South Carolina.

It's so pretty here, I thought, looking into the green thickets surrounding the entrance gate. I caught a whiff of what I thought was honeysuckle in the wind.

But the buildings, I thought, have got to go. I stared down the grim, gray boxlike structures until it became apparent I was supposed to go into one, the one with all the flags standing in gold tubes beside the doors. The ten of us from the bus nosed our way timidly to the front desk, where a short black man in a fiercely stiff uniform made all the new arrivals sit cross-legged on the floor with our traveling packs for an hour and a half. "Hurry up and wait" is a well-known army routine, and we found it exemplified several different times that day. We'd be doing something, say, going to the bathroom, or organizing our wall lockers, and suddenly a sergeant would yell at us to get our sorry butts downstairs for roll call. We'd stop mid-task and scramble recklessly through hallways the color of Deep Shit and out to the squares of pavement in the courtyard where they'd line us up and call our last names. Then we'd stand there. And stand there. We'd shift our weight from foot to foot, crack jokes, get yelled at for cracking jokes, and finally they'd tell us to go upstairs and shut up.

Well, I thought that first night, curling up under my olive drab wool blanket, punching up a pancake-flat pillow, listening to the chatter of the other women and the squeaks of their bunk springs, if this is it, I'll be fine. It's inefficient, yes, but not horrible.

That first week, we did mundane things like uniform fittings, vaccinations, gear gathering. Command had given us a forward on our first paychecks, so we could go to the BX (Base Exchange), kind of like Walmart, and buy the requisite things: plain white unsexy underpants, gym shoes, sports bras, heel supports and ankle braces, army stationery with the lone soldier walking across each page, teeth guards, ChapStick, watch, and backup watch (if you lose track of the time, they told us, you will be FUBAR—Fucked Up Beyond All Recognition)! They gave us our handy army training manuals containing all the rules, symbols, and acronyms we needed to know, and some handy adages, like "Freedom isn't free."

Then they fed us our last meal at the main mess hall, where there was, to everyone's surprise, an ice cream machine.

The following morning, our first morning of "real" basic training, the drill sergeants came blasting into our bunks with whistles at 5 a.m. and shouted at us to grab our pre-packed duffel bags and run down to the bus dock. They crammed us into a fleet of white buses and took us deeper into Fort Jackson, away from the entrance gate we could still see opening and closing with each busload during those first few days. At the head of each bus, a mean-looking drill sergeant maintained silence, simply by standing and staring back at us.

As a child, I'd lived with my family in rural Kentucky, in a large house with two back decks that overlooked a thirty-foot ravine. When my brother and I peered down into it, it seemed more like seventy-five feet deep. The sides of it, which started their descent from neighboring yards and an adjacent cow field, sloped down at 45-degree angles, providing a habitat for trees, blankets of variegated leaves, rocks, and in the winter, mud. My brother Bobey and I would gain permission to go missing for an hour at a time and clamber, half walking and half sliding, down the walls to the creek bed at the bottom. We'd walk along the banks away from the house, hiding in the root balls of trees that were upturned by yearly tornado gusts, picking out bugs: fat, white beetle larvae, silken-winged moths, spiders of all shapes and sizes, most of them furry.

We dug with sticks to find arrowheads, trillium fossils, and rough geodes that contained crystals when you cracked them open on larger rocks.

We played with the sticks, imagining they were swords, the same way we imagined our stuffed animals were alive, sailing the world's hidden seas as we scooted them in shoe boxes across the seafoam green carpet upstairs.

Beve, the cleverly named stuffed beaver with the Scottish-plaid replacement tail ("It was all the fabric I had left!" Mum said), was the imaginative manifestation of myself. He would go on all the adventures I, as a parentally protected kid, could not. He went sailing, spelunking, surfing (learning how to hang ten), owned a scooter, fought with pirates, conducted peacemaking ceremonies with other animals from faraway islands, and made love with Lizzie the Fat Brown Beaver on a regular basis. Sometimes Beve would come with Bobey and me in a little backpack when we traversed the ravine.

One day, for some reason, no one was paying attention and the three of us, Bobey and Beve and I, walked farther back than we had ever been. We rounded an unfamiliar rocky bend to find a burial mound in the middle of the creek. Stopped instantly, we craned our necks, then drew a little closer, looking at the shape of it. Large white sandstones were piled in a human-sized oval, a giant half-egg in the middle of the water. Two sticks, lashed into a bony cross, pointed skyward out of the center of it.

"Bet it's just a dog," Bobe said.

Beve and I looked on silently. I thought maybe one of the neighboring hillbillies had shot his cousin and sunk the body in the creek, under the rocks, where it would crumble apart and follow the trickling water down into Tennessee.

"Let's go back," I said. "I'm getting the creeps."

"Me too," said Bobe.

Joining the army reserves was something like that, something reminiscent of that feeling that you wanted an adventure, you called it down upon yourself, but maybe you opened the door a little too far. I think many people have this feeling at one point or another. You walk into your teenage boyfriend's house one day after school and see his friends cutting coke on the living room coffee table. Mike, the one with the freckles and crystalline blue eyes, sees you, holds up the mirror.

"Want some?"

You stand there in the doorway, not sure whether to be the saucy sixteen-year-old who rolls with anything or whether to paddle backwards shyly into the driveway. Whatever you choose, you never have the choice to unsee Mike with the straw, snuffing the powder sharply up into his mind. Whatever light illuminates that strange new place will etch something of its own into you.

The first day at "real" basic training, we learned several important things.

We learned to say, "Sir yes sir," "Ma'am yes ma'am," and "Drill Sergeant, yes Drill Sergeant" to every order issued to us, and otherwise not to get caught speaking.

We learned to eat our meals in three minutes flat. We learned that if you didn't eat enough, you'd get weak and sickly before the next meal, since the army, unlike an airline, does not offer midday snacks.

We learned to sleep through loud snoring in giant, sterile rooms called bays, where bodies tightly lined the walls in metal bunk beds at night.

We learned to organize all our gear in our wall lockers, and to exist with no personal effects besides ChapStick and an army notepad for letter writing. The letter writing would be done at night in the latrines, while you pretended to shit, because the slender hour of "personal time" given at the end of each day was frequently spent shining boots and fighting ten other naked bodies for water in the shower. The water was never warm, but everyone craved it anyway, desperate to wash away their new outdoorsy army fragrance.

In addition to all this, we learned that if you disobeyed the drill sergeants in any manner, you could end up doing push-ups until you vomited. Or, worse, you might end up like Private Kilm, who was made to do push-ups with sandbags on his back, and who ended up in the clinic.

We usually exercised at least twice per day, not counting the numerous improvised "smoke sessions" we accepted as minor punishments for minor fuck-ups. The "real" exercise sessions were called PT, for physical training. We put on our gray-and-black army regulation shorts, T-shirts, and tennis shoes for this, and they ran us five miles, or took us to the gym. Other times we wore full BDUs (battle dress uniforms, otherwise known as fatigues, complete with cloppy black boots) and did a tactical practice, like running through the woods with a backpack, or climbing and rappelling a tower. Those weren't so bad. The smoke sessions were, on the other hand, sneaky and brutal, and usually enacted for something you didn't know you'd done wrong.

I was the first of our platoon to receive a smoking, on the first day. The sun was wicked strong for early April, and the sweat accumulating on my nose was catching the weight of the heavy brown-framed spectacles, pulling them down to the end of my nose. We were standing at attention—body tall and still, arms flanked to the waist, eyes forward, and you can't move!—and I snuck my hand up quick to push the glasses back up.

"HEY! PRIVATE! WHY DID YOU MOVE! I JUST SAW YOU MOVE!"

Drill Sergeant Lamartine was a lean, wiry woman whose eyes seemed to pop from her head, and they glinted down to my nametag.

"GET ON THE GROUND PAAR!"

I got down.

"IN THE PUSH-UP POSITION PAAR!"

I groaned on the inside.

"Now hold it," she said, not quite yelling anymore. She went on to explain the rules for attention posture to the rest of the platoon. My arms started to wobble. Habitual smoking and inactivity made my lungs quiver for air.

"NOW PAAR," she said, returning to me, "we're going to have a little demonstration."

"Drill Sergeant, yes Drill Sergeant!"

"What?"

"DRILL SERGEANT, YES DRILL SERGEANT!"

"PUSH!!"

I pushed down onto my hands so my fingers began to bend up at the middle knuckles, then pushed my weight up, grinding the bases of my hands into all the little pebbles on the pavement.

Push down, breathe.

Push up. Exhale, and let the air of my lungs out into the wavy heat.

Eventually, they would teach us how to say different things between counts, to help with our breathing, I assumed. Things like this:

Drill Sergeant: DOWN!
Us: ONE!
Drill Sergeant: UP!
Us: MAKE IT HURT DRILL SERGEANT, MAKE IT HURT!

And other similarly encouraging expressions. One remarkably memorable one was a cadence, a marching song, that we would repeat in chorus after the drill sergeant's lead while our ill-fitting boots clopped along the pavement into an echo. In a mass of unified voices, we would yell: "A little bird / with a yellow bill / was sitting on / my windowsill. / I lured him in / with a piece of bread / and then I crushed / his little head."

By the third week into it, getting an average four hours of sleep per night, waking up to whistles and shouted insults each morning, finding new torture each day to write home in letters to friends, I felt as though maybe we, the trainees, were the little birds in this equation.

Sergeant Driver, my bald and cheerful recruiter from 12th and Broadway in Northeast Portland, had convinced me the army was less sexist than most other American employers. And I responded well to this lure: there'd been many times growing up when I'd felt my "girlness" impeded my capacity for adventure and inclusion. I would wish upon the plenitude of stars in our backyard to be transformed overnight into a boy, or at least to be recognized by the world as competent like a boy, while I kept my own ladylike mind and long legs. That way, I could do fun things like running, wrestling, and shooting guns, instead of the hateful things to which I, and not my brother, was annoyingly subjected: babysitting, cooking, having to sit and chat with adults while the boys played video games, endlessly listening to other girls converse about weight and makeup, watching my prepubescent friends pretend their dolls were children.

Once, when I was ten, my dad's three brothers came over to our house. They drank cold Olympia beer out of the stacks of cases we kept in the basement vault, and threw the baseball. We hauled giant sticks out of the slanted corn patch that my dad had decided, for some reason, to sow on a hill. We ate bologna sandwiches and Lay's chips for lunch. Then we swung on the creaky vine that arced out over the ravine, and shot the aforementioned beer cans off a tree stump from the back deck, or shot at paper target politicians my dad thought were terrorists.

"Why don't you go help your mom with dinner?" Dad asked when the sky began to yellow.

"I don't want to," I said. My turn to shoot was coming up. I was eyeballing Arafat.

"That's okay. You can do it anyway," he said, and patted me on the shoulder.

So I stalked upstairs. Stirred some beans in a pot. We ate, then I got to help clean up. When I went back downstairs, my dad, my uncles, and my brother were all working on my favorite puzzle, the one that depicted a medieval town in England, with a billion things happening at once: a dirty peasant throwing a pail of poop out a window, a bunch of dough-faced children climbing around on a dead horse, and a red-nosed dunce pushing a huge stein deep down into a giant, frothy keg of beer. By the time I joined them, my brother had already done the whole border, my favorite part.

That fall, my mom got us a membership at the Elizabethtown Swim and Fitness Center. My brother and I played basketball while she worked out in the gym. The redheaded boy on whom I had a crush couldn't get around me to the hoop. I smiled secretly, thinking he might admire my ability as a ballplayer. I matched him step for step. Maybe, I thought, if I steal the ball from him, he'll be enchanted and kiss me. But I couldn't steal the ball from him, and he couldn't score. We were all locked up. Finally he stopped, picked up the ball, and yelled, "Get off me, you psycho Barbie!"

I wanted to crawl into a hole. I wondered if anyone would ever appreciate the fact that I was not a Barbie, not really even a girl in the traditional cheerleadery sense. That I wanted a very different kind of existence.

Although Sergeant Driver wasn't entirely right about the equal-opportunity nature of the army, at least most of the time the chain of command treated all the trainees like equal puddles of pond scum. About a week or two after we arrived, two of the female drill sergeants took the women from my platoon into a large ladies' latrine and gave us a talking-to about what it means to be a female in the military. They were the buggy-eyed one and the one who wore makeup and never raised her voice. ("If I get to the point of yelling, I'll just smoke you," she used to say calmly.)

What they said went like this: Don't fraternize with the males, for *fuck's sake* don't *sit* on the toilet seats, always wash your hands, eat extra food during your period, and if your period stops, it's normal with all the PT we've been doing, so don't worry about it. At the end of this "discussion," I had to admit, I started to feel like they cared about us especially; here they were, taking their time to forewarn us about the dangers of STDs, the ways our particular bodies would change, and disciplinary trouble with boys. At the end of it, though, the makeup-wearing drill sergeant stood up, put her finger to the corner of her plum-colored lips and said, "Now, get on the ground." And they had us do push-ups for half an hour, right there in the powder-blue latrine together, our hands pressed at odd, cramped angles on the tiles.

At the same time that our unit began to get used to the grim monotony of basic training, other moments became memorable against the swirl of routine:

The Alpha Pathfinder platoon learned how to belay and rappel. We ran beforehand, a tactical run, scattered across a thicket, one soldier every few paces, through the wood to the field station where our drill would be conducted.

There, in the ground next to a narrow pine tree, hid a gnarled brown root. It hadn't moved in years, and water had rushed below the center of it, making the root into a kind of trap for the toes of combat boots. I saw it just before it grabbed me and took me chin-to-ground. My glasses had gone flying, and I would be screwed if I didn't get them before they were crushed. But when I tried to pull myself up to scramble for them, I realized I couldn't really move. Then I realized I couldn't really breathe, but there was a drill sergeant coming, so I had to move. I felt myself inhale sharply as I was pulled up from behind by my ammo belt. The pressure on my chest vanished. Someone had got hold of me, and as I was returned to a flat-footed stand I realized it was Private Neil's giant-sized hand on my left shoulder, righting me.

"You okay?"

"Glasses!" I stuttered, and he leaned over to lift them out of the leaves.

"Thanks, man."

"Yeah, you okay?"

"I think so."

"Try and jog, then."

I tried. I could do it a little. My lungs felt a little like a bellows stuck shut. I wondered if I'd popped a hole. I pictured a sharp little fragment of bone poking right against the snot-slick surface, turning pink to red. I'd be spitting up blood in a minute if that was the case.

Suck. Go. Suck. Go. Get the rhythm. Bend the pain.

Neil was at my side and gave me a knowing smile.

"What?" I gasped, mildly irritated.

"You all the same, you city kids. You startle real quick, but you'll be juss fine. Don't worry." Voice like molasses, stereotypical of the South, and not less soothing because of it. A lot of recruits were southern, and some, like Neil, had kind southern manners.

"Okay."

"C'mon."

We bumbled out of the woods into the clearing. Thin camel-colored dirt made a circle around a very tall wooden tower. Splintery timber had been nailed into a rough, wide ladder ascending to the top of the structure, reminding me of a tree house we had in Kentucky, amplified in height. Soldiers colored it in green spots as they ascended. Neil left my side to venture forward and up, and I stood in awe, watching this massive anthill of activity. I stood, and then I moved.

"Think like an ant!" I told myself.

I made my antly way forward to the wood sculpture, legs marching automatically. Up I climbed, wincing into the ladder when I used my left arm or bent any portion of my chest forward. Fragments of wood drove into my palms. At the top, the view was dizzying. I turned my head and looked sideways out at the field. Drill Sergeant Mako, whose teeth hardly fit into his head, rendering him sharklike, yelled at me to get my ass to the rappel point. So I did, crossing the top of the tower by shuffling across a narrow walkway that led to a gaping hole in the center. Rope netting had been built into this hole, suspended above nothing, and I clambered onto it. My body, if the netting should break, would fall fifty or so feet onto the dust patch beneath. But the blue plastic ropes held fast, and I crawled across the weblike suspension to reach the drill sergeant. He barely looked at me as he clipped me into a harness. I looked out at all the little soldiers running around below, the plush green forest top, the distant hills.

Everything was easy to see, but with less sound. Then I turned around, extended both legs to the tower's flat rappelling wall, and leaned back into nothingness. Mako the Shark started to lower me downward. I could hear the squeak of another blue rope, threading through a pulley, growing more distant as I made my floating descent. I looked out at the field again, a few strands of hair escaping my helmet and hovering in the unsteady breeze as my body felt equally spacetime-suspended. It was like riding on a sigh. I watched everything on the ground grow closer, as the sky shrank back again. Pretty soon I could recognize the people in the uniforms.

The following day, I gained permission to go to the hospital on the troop bus. I told the medic, who seemed like an amateur, about my ribs. He assured me they were merely bruised. He gave me Motrin to reduce inflammation. I got a permission slip to take a week off push-ups. Then I was back to full duty, and I used only my right arm to pull myself out of my bunk in the morning, weaving my fingers into the springs on the bottom of Webster's bed for leverage.

Another day, we were in the field, the sun steaming down my back. I stood across from Private Vargas in a line, and we held our bayonets while shouting at each other, "KILL!"

Or, alternately, "KILL, KILL, KILL WITHOUT MERCY!!"

Turn. "KILL!"

Turn again. "KILL!"

Vargas was a joker with a ready smirk, from a barrio, Catholic, and maybe he thought this was as unrelated to real living as I did, so we grinned and played macho as we killed each other. Let's kill each other, you know, like let's do lunch.

Hey, Vargas, turn and "KILL!!!!!" Then we combed ourselves into a single line and awaited our turns to stab the dummy.

The dummy.

Pasty pale white canvas.

No face.

No weapon.

Just a fake person on a pole. But when I rushed it, when I put my knife into this stuffed, weak, inanimate thing, with all the power my arms, my head, my legs, my grinding teeth could afford, suddenly, part of me dropped out of myself.

Right there, suddenly, in the middle of the field, I felt sick.

I wanted to lean on my weapon.

I wanted to feel it catch me in the spine like a fish on a campfire stick.

Maybe someone, maybe Vargas, could come and stand me up in the field like a scarecrow. All the other soldiers could watch me, understand what a devil I was. What an angel and a devil I was, torn in two, sliding wetly down my bayonet, and what they were too: people willing to break through the ribs of another creature, just because someone else told us, and was paying us all, to do it.

I questioned, then, the idea itself of patriotism: What made my country better than another, if our lofty principles, like so many other ordinary countries', could founder on the practice of killing and controlling others to preserve it?

But I would suffocate this feeling and play it cool: I was surrounded by wannabe warriors. Play it cool like the small, dim brick building that housed the gas.

"Wear the mask in," the drill sergeants said, as we lined up outside, "then take off the mask. Say the ABCs. You have to say the complete alphabet before we'll let you out, and you can't drop your mask."

I thought this was a stupid comment, and I said so to Private Burk, who snickered. Who, after all, would drop a piece of military uniform in front of the five drill sergeants that would be in there with us? Bad move! Lots of push-ups! We filed in and removed our masks in the hazy little room. I wondered, before my eyes clouded with water, whether the green came from the gas or whether it was actually a special effect, some trick of light, generated just for the psychologically sickening effect it had on us. There was a lonely light bulb in the corner of the room, in a cage. Perhaps that was the trickery.

"Abcdefghijklmnopqrstuvwxyz," I said so fast I impressed even myself. Then the drill sergeant said, "No, stupid, the army alphabet." She was fucking serious, and this was suddenly a problem.

"Alpha, beta, gamma, delta, epsilon . . ."

No, I thought, that was Greek.

"Alpha, Bravo, Charlie, Delta, Echo, Foxtrot, Golf, . . ." I struggled along then, sinuses filling with mucus, knowing I'd start gagging any second. I stopped for a coughing fit halfway through, which caused me to suck the poisoned oxygen in even faster, even deeper. My ribs, if they weren't cracked before, were by now. I finished, to the astonishment of Drill Sergeant Hector, who applauded and said, "Now get out, stupid." I ran outside as fast as I could, lines of snot oozing down my cheeks into my mouth, and right outside the door I dropped my mask.

For atomic bomb training, I thought we'd get some kind of high-tech mask, but we didn't. It was only two minutes long:

you lie flat on your stomach with your head facing the direction of the "boom" that represents detonation. This way, the rush of atomic wind that follows won't blow your head off your neck and disassemble your skeleton. I wondered, if a person could see anything during a nuclear holocaust, how many heads she might see whizzing down the street.

"PAAR! YOU'RE FACIN' THE WRONG WAY!! BETTER ROLL OVER! MEDITATE, COCKROACH STYLE!"

I turned over, lay on my back, boots high above me, and did crunches while bicycling my legs. Although this exercise was a punishment for facing the wrong direction during the drill, I liked it, for the posture gave me a chance to admire the short-cut grass wiggling like tiny fingertips in the wind. I could breathe the smell of it in, as deep into my lungs as they'd open: the frank odor of pollen, the scent of growth amidst the gray smoke of the bomb simulator. At this moment I was happy to be a cockroach lying upside down on my shell. For one thing, the cockroach is one of the only animals some scientists predict could ever survive a nuclear holocaust, which made me feel strong. At the same time, flipped over, belly up, I could feel the sun on my stomach again, soothing me, simply and kindly, into the deep, archaic pleasure of warmth.

About eight weeks into basic, we went on a tactical march at midnight through a high-altitude pine forest. It was a half-moon sky, bright enough to see the pale pine needles against the blue-white dirt. The trees seemed like pale skeletons, rising thinly from this supernatural carpet.

As we walked, speechlessly, in a long single line, I could hear so many things: boots crunching into gravel, crickets, mysterious bush-rustling, a lone owl calling.

The world was coming in at the skin.

And I found myself enchanted with that moment that only the few of us together would know and understand, and I understood why some people stay in the army after all the other sane ones leave: you get these pieces of experience that are special, that much of humanity will never know. You walk purposely forward into the unknown, directed by the hands of the military gods, ready for anything and willing as lambs on a slab of ultimate surrender. Masochists of the S&M scene, I found out later, often say there is no greater freedom than that which is locked inside your voluntary surrender to bondage. Also, ironically, here, there is no greater sense of yourself than when you're a part of a massive organized creature working toward a common end.

I felt, then, like I got it. I got it all. Epiphany in a late-frosted coniferous tree line.

And then I felt too, suddenly, a snag in my pelvis pulling insistently down, like part of me might clatter out, right there, onto the dirt.

I knew something was wrong. I knew I needed medical attention, and I knew I needed it soon.

Later that week, I got my appointment.

I went to the hospital, this time to a greasy-haired captain who asked me if I was malingering (faking sick, which, in the military, is a crime).

"Says here you've been in three times already in two months."

"Yessir," I say. "Twice for my ribs and once when I needed cough drops."

"Paar, I don't know what you've got going, if you're just a weakling or what, but I suggest you buck up. You have another three weeks before AIT. If you go to PTRP now, you'll seriously regret it."

AIT was Advanced Individual Training, where I'd learn how to fulfill the thrilling task of acting as Fort Lewis's newest "supply specialist" back in Washington state. PTRP was the Physical Training and Rehabilitation Program, and, as I'd heard from the many whispering voices of the barracks, it was a cesspool of a company where soldiers got stuck for long periods of time.

"You've pulled a muscle." The sweaty captain handed me an Ace bandage. "Wrap it."

The next day I wrapped my thigh and ran five miles.

Private Webster, a dork similar to me in dress and demeanor, was, as I've said, my battle buddy. Everyone had one. You could never be alone in basic training, just like you could never be alone in battle, for reasons of safety. If I got smoked for something I did, she did my push-ups with me, and vice versa. We knew how to tighten each other's glasses straps.

One night we had fireguard duty, an annoying task that cut two hours out of an already slim six-hour nightly sleep allotment. After counting the heads of everyone in our bay to guarantee against runaways, we sat in the fold-up metal chairs at the building entrance, watching mosquito eaters tap their legs against the amber light of the barracks' glass doors. Webster yawned, and opened her arms in a great stretch toward the ceiling. I yawned too, and winced when I tried to lift my arms. I'd forgotten about the ribs.

"How are they doing?" she said. "Lemme see."

I looked around and peeled up my BDU top gingerly.

"Don't touch 'em!" I warned.

"God, they look like shit!" she exclaimed. "They look lopsided. You need to go back to the hospital!"

"They told me they're not busted," I said.

"Well, they're wrong. Get an X-ray. You can tell them about your pelvis, too. Look, you can barely walk."

Webster'd been a nurse-in-training in her civilian life, and her suggestion seemed sound. I went back that week to the hospital, got X-rays, and was found to have two fractured ribs, a fractured pelvis, and a fractured femur.

They sent me to PTRP.

At this PTRP there were many soldiers with not a lot to do but wait, competing for space and privileges, and people didn't seem to make it out of there very fast. The rumor was that people couldn't heal. When I arrived, there was an ambulance and a stain on the pavement below the bay balcony; apparently someone had thrown himself off. The longer I stayed there, the more I understood why: waiting for hours for meals in formation on crutches, verbal abuse without the possibility of attaining any goal or eventually receiving praise, soldiers stuck there so long their hope had turned to cruelty.

I didn't know anyone except Smith and two other privates from my platoon who got broken at the same time. We sat on the grill-hot pavement and waited. Most days, we all sat around and did nothing but light exercises on an ugly blue mat and avoided the male soldiers who wanted to take us below the stairs into the "boom boom room." No one was allowed to talk much, or read, or write. Just stretch and do leg lifts, which hurt my ribs. And everyone was back-bitey. Someone stole my CDs. There was talk of "shower parties" (barracks beatings), and I watched a giant ape of a soldier pretend to mouth-fuck a girl in my bunk, holding her by the pigtails, shoving his still-clothed pelvis at her protesting face. And I met Private Loid, who had lived at PTRP for two years, or so she said, with her knees not healing, away from husband and family. She planned to sue when she got discharged.

Before this time, I'd rarely felt suicidal. But like on bayonet day, I found myself wishing I still had my rifle. I could talk to the hole in my rifle. It would understand this madness, though no one else seemed to. I was supposed to start school in three weeks, without my reserve status or my GI Bill. When I went to the unit "counselor" to tell him about all this, his reply was "I don't give a shit about your school, Private. Get your ass back to training and out of my face."

I sat on the hot pavement that evening during roll call, thinking. Jeers and obscenities scraped through the air around me. I decided to hunt down Private Brooks, who went AWOL to go to the beach for two days, then came back to the unit. I wanted to ask about consequences. I found him at the front desk, where he served his extra duty, every morning and every night, while the rest of the company would sleep or stretch.

"Yeah, they tell you that they'll throw you in prison," he said, scratching a tiny insect out of his hair, "but when I came back, they just yelled at me, then asked me if I wanted to stay or not. I said yes."

"What the fuck is wrong with you?" I said, my voice suddenly loud. Green-collared necks turned.

"What? I just wanted a break." He laughed, then noticed my expression.

"Paar," he said quietly, pulling me away toward the door, "if you want out of this, go now. There won't always be a loophole."

He circled his finger around his head, pointing it in the direction of the command station across the quad.

"You know how we've had these inspections lately?" he said.

I nodded, imagining the last dog and pony show we put on when the colonel from Fort Bragg walked through, us all quiet, well groomed, under the dagger eyes of our sergeants.

"Some people don't think this place is run right. Command is nervous. They're gonna be tightening the rules every day. No more trips to the hospital without direct supervision. Head counts every hour."

I felt my throat drop into my stomach. I was too numb, right then, even to vomit.

This girl's American Dream, I thought, has become a nightmare from which I cannot wake.

I paced around the women's bay for the rest of the afternoon, studying the brick walls, the metal bunks, the small screen-covered windows near the ceiling of every chambered room.

I remembered this feeling, in a smaller way, years before. After my parents divorced, they split custody, but it drove each of them crazy. Mum eventually moved us back to Portland, where we'd been born, and we saw Dad summers in Kentucky. One summer, he lived at a lake house. He was unhappy thinking about us leaving again and made a comment: "I should have taken you both and gone off into the woods. They'd never find us."

But I didn't want to live in the woods and not see Mum. So I studied the way the main road was from the lake, knew which window I could open and drop down from without hurting myself, knew where the crunchy gravel and the motion light stopped against the quiet edge of darkness, which I could use as cover, taking Bobey with me, if we needed to go. I was a good hider: I could be small. In hide-and-seek with the cousins, I won by squeezing myself into the thin standing shower and leaving the curtain mostly open, fooling the other kids by becoming a sliver of myself.

I can do this, I thought. I'm built, after all, not to kill, but to flee.

I fingered the lock on my wall locker thinking: If I left my unit and was caught, the MPs would handcuff me and return me to a squad of circling drill sergeants, lieutenants, and captains I had no desire to ever encounter one-on-one. They would give me extra duty and fireguard every night until I had no time to think about anything else, ever again. If I left and was not immediately caught, I might have to live out my life in Mexico, Canada, South America someplace, alone. But, if Brooks was right, would they negotiate with me, if I just made myself too much trouble to keep? The damage potential of a dishonorable discharge terrified: jail, joblessness, difficulty renting. Not to mention shame from two sides of my family both marbled with military. The only thing I knew was that if I left at night, they would send the MPs out as soon as I came up gone for head count, which would only give me an hour to get off base. I had to leave during the day, between lunch mess and dinner mess, when I would have at least three hours to get a start, before they'd count heads and miss me, before hell came pounding after me.

So, that very same night, I got out of bed late and went to the latrine with my brown BDU shirt. I was dizzy with fear and fatigue. The room was empty and bright, and noiseless except for cicada calls echoing through the bays of sleeping bodies. I plugged the sink with a twist of paper towel and found the bleach we used for mopping.

"Freedom is not worth having if it does not include the freedom to make mistakes," I told myself. Thanks, Gandhi!

Then I uncapped the bleach. It ran in rivulets into my shirt, and I watched the fabric reincarnate from shit brown to robin's egg blue.

The Cockroach Prayer—39

The next morning, I pulled the shirt gingerly under my army logo sweatshirt, careful not to bump my ribs. I checked out my medical file and signed out before head count to the clinic. Rumors flew it was the last day we would be allowed to sign out alone. This day, instead of getting off the bus at the clinic, I pulled the cord to get off one stop early, at the BX. The driver, a suspicious old army retiree, looked my haphazard uniform up and down and said nothing. As the bus pulled away, I pulled the sweatshirt over my head and walked, heart bellowing, past the military police to the taxicabs parked at the edge of the parking lot. I prayed to look like a civilian. I prayed to be invisible. With all the might in my little cockroach mind, I said: *Let me out. You have to let me out!*

At the cab, the door sucked shut.

"Greyhound station," I said.

I would escah-pay from this great big mistah-kay.

I had to be the yellow bird that lived.

The rest of that madness was a blur to me then, and is still now. I found the Greyhound station crawling with military personnel, so I took off my standard-issue glasses and squinted hard at departure timetables, the insignia on camouflage-clad breasts and sleeves—a blind person trying to lead myself to light.

I stood for a moment in the fray. A mean-looking commander of some sort was standing near me, and I could tell he was looking at me. My hand itched to salute. My back was starting to straighten into an attention posture or parade rest, but I realized, quickly, I shouldn't do anything.

"Don't look for the stripes," I schooled myself. "A civilian would treat a captain just like a sergeant or, just like another human being. Be a civilian again."

So I ignored the mean-looking commander until he looked human again, and eventually he walked back over to his troops. I took a place in the ticket line, and looked forward.

"Portland, Oregon," I said to the blurry woman at the counter. After that, my memory goes patchy:

The green muddle of foliage out the window gradually fading to night.

The constant hum of wheels beneath me.

A slanted stretch of land with hot licks of fire flashing forth from tall towers.

A minor accident on the way to Louisville, the bus having sideswiped a small commuter car.

My pulse began to race, and I walked back to the bus's bathroom vowing: if the cops come on board, even if it's just to check that the passengers are okay, I will climb down into this toilet and hide until they are gone.

In Louisville I stopped to stay with an old friend, did a little research about what to do.

When I called the GI hotline, they told me to wait thirty days to change my status to "deserter" and then turn myself in at Fort Knox. I was to take the bus back, not a plane, because I needed to turn myself in as a gesture of lawfulness, rather than letting the MPs find me first.

"How do I know they won't put me in jail anyway?" I said.

"This is the best information we have right now," replied the calm, anonymous woman.

I arrived another three days later back in Portland and slept on the floor of another friend's house, where no one in the army would think to find me.

My sergeants from PTRP called my mom's house, looking.

Each night, I dreamt of drill sergeants.

But I wasn't done yet; I had to go back.

I was meant to start school at the end of August. If I went to Fort Knox for a week, I'd miss a week of classes. If I went to Fort Knox and they kept me, or if I got caught at school later, that would be that. I imagined the massive gold vaults I saw as a child on a school tour in Fort Knox, how they must also have prison cells ready-made for an escapee like me, an AWOL private, a pond scum, a nobody that nobody would miss if she were quietly locked away into the dark. And yet this risk of imprisonment was the most likely path to freedom again. My body, mind: both felt like just pain containers now anyway.

So fuck it.

The bus was a rolling, soaring tuna can, carrying me back across the country.

At every break I stepped out to chain-smoke, while around me insects rasped. I tried to memorize calm, in case the woman on the hotline was wrong and they kept me. I wanted to know that my hand-lotion smelled like vanilla, that my ChapStick tasted like lemonade, how the sky folded together in three layers of auburn in evening. I wanted to know what the long and infinite highway looked like, cased in varied textures of pavement, in case I didn't see a road again for a long, long time.

Then I arrived at Fort Knox. I stepped off the bus, walked past two enthusiastic trainees discussing beer and cunts. I put one foot in front of the other, walked up to the building, put out my last cigarette, and entered.

After about a week of polishing floors and paperwork, I could leave.

When the Twin Towers fell, I thought they'd call me back, but they didn't, and the unit I was originally meant to join in Washington, I heard, went to Afghanistan without me. My nightmares went on for some years, and I quit school again, but nobody ever came knocking for me, and eventually I began to understand that no one would. Slowly I could begin to refashion my future. I wish I could say the process by which I recovered my life was tidy, or steady, or discernible, but it wasn't. I did a lot of strange things trying to scrape images of faux mouth-fucking, sandbag push-ups, and bayonets off the backs of my eyelids.

But here I am. Alive. Shell intact.

Sometimes, if I'm lucky, I can peek out, take off my shell for a minute, and place it over to the side. I can feel the respiration of the world around me, sucking in, pushing out. I can feel it thrumming in my guts. And I know that even I, tiniest of creatures, have a place in the warmth of its hurricane breathing.

Some nights, knowing this, I even sleep well: not an atomic wind could wake me.

Formula

You all went to school with me, full of plaid clothes and right answers.

Most of us complained about it then—the rules, the dogma, the ritual—but many of you stayed in the Church afterward: married each other out of high school up at the altars, made families and took them to Mass, sent your kids to the same Catholic schools we attended, where Mrs. Lewis told us to do our math homework or end up in hell.

I think I found math, and perhaps Mrs. Lewis's philosophy, harder than most of you: pushing my glasses up on my nose and scribbling "8 + 2" over and over onto the quiz slip until Sister Mary Something called time, as if by simply retracing the components I was given I'd eventually get the right answer to fall magically into the blank. I disliked these maneuvers of subtracting and summing, compounding and dividing. Then fractions, exponents . . . opportunities to get the answers wrong compounding.

However, the formula offered in religion class was simple, and I secretly liked that: that the omnipresence who'd made us would love us if we just did our best to be nice. And if we screwed this up—say, we gossiped or smacked someone for gossiping about us—all we had to do was apologize (to our peers, and then to God himself in the wooden confessional box), and we could start afresh, a messy blackboard erased.

Little Me pictured "God" as an accumulation of wind who smiled.

He/She/It felt like a more lax and generous compilation of parts and structures than those of our parents, whose love could seem to run out after 7 p.m., or after about seven beers. God makes exceptions to his rules, wonderfully unpredictably: welcoming back the sinning prodigal son, the prostitutes, letting Jesus flip some tables over in anger at the temple-gone-marketplace.

The nuns at my first Catholic school, devoted to discerning the Trinity's unusual trigonometry, took us kids on nature walks (where I imagined the Holy Spirit lived), to Mass where we could sing, and then in a solemn group to the wall where we could stroll along the morbid but somehow calming stations of the cross: watch Jesus drag his heavy wood burden and die on it over and over again to set us free from the traps of our own flesh-bound foibles.

Jesus, Himself a splinter of Wind-friend who'd wrapped Himself in skin like ours, gave clear examples of how to behave during conflict: conflict, of course, created because you have a body. Because particles collide.

"You must love your enemy."

This simple-sounding edict was complex, for it implied that even if someone harms you, you must again offer them your vulnerability: "Turn the other cheek."

The vulnerability, it seems, could act as invitation: to show that pain can be surmounted. That it was possible to roll our splintered units of self back together again against the force of our fracture (a garden, a tree, a snake).

Formula (noun): from the Latin *forma* (to make), as God made us by breathing into dirt ("male and female created he them").

I saw us all trying: pantomiming players of holiness in our Christmas nativity plays.

We left room for the Holy Ghost between our bodies at school dances.

We eavesdropped on each other's sins through the confessional box wall: we stole from our sisters and lied about chores.

Then we brought our kneelers clunking down together.

At Mass we salivated for the wafer, then the more flavorful wine.

In these equations, solving for love, for alignment with the divine, was always the goal.
 $8 + 2 = $ love.
 Hardship plus faith equals love.
 Cruelty plus patience and forgiveness equals love.
 There were tough variables, of course: the urge to lash out after embarrassment, anger at being told what to do, human ego and frailty.
 Yet despite these struggles, just one refrain: caring as constant solution.

Because of this, Little Me ached to live in a peaceful cloister, sleep in a quiet, Spartan room. She wished to wear a simple habit and marry the Godly Wind person, the Good News, the ubiquitous goal of a better human world. These were, perhaps, wildly romantic ideas for a pre-sexual child: heroic, the stuff of picture books.
 But could you blame her? In the saint books we studied during library class, raptly turning page after page, we could see how the most dedicated Christians, the saints, were willing to do anything, even cancel out their own lives, to prove the universal equation of love can work.
 There was Lucy, eyes removed unkindly.
 Saint Stephen, double martyred with stones after being shot with arrows.
 Saint Valentine, who, we discovered, fell in love with his jailer's daughter and, before his beheading, sent her a note signed "from your Valentine," rendering romance and respectability unifiable.

My favorite saint was Joan of Arc, whose passion for compassion led her to donning men's clothes and charging bravely forward in battle. It did not occur to me, then, that this act was the opposite of employing our "turn the other cheek" mantra: she was canonized, and her violence had been called "righteous" by Church leaders who knew (and still do) more than me.

So, in the park across from our house, I'd sit alone on a swing while my mom and brother played in piles of leaves nearby, and I'd gather little symbols into my hands to pose for my own future saint picture: a red five-armed maple like a little blood-red battle flag, a stone for steadfastness, and a tiny spiny walnut pod, just like Saint Joan of Arc's flail.

When the boys in our class, newly testosteroned, began to pick on my friends—flirt-chasing Beth on the playground or flicking gum at Jenny—Little Me followed Joan's example and fought back "righteously," kicking Todd in the nuts, shoving Alex's head into the right-angle corner of a desk. Of course, she took home pink slips instead of praise for defending her friends the victims of these pint-sized aggressions. School, she would soon learn, was not the place for righteous violence: the military was. And women, though allowed in the military, were not really meant for fighting. Years after childhood, Young Woman Me would join the army: partly to pay for some college education and partly because it seemed like an easy way to be right. In basic, where she changed her mind about this, command wanted everyone at church on Sundays; she'd become agnostic, in a spiritual but solitary way, and would stay in the bay to read. When enough of the other trainees discovered that this loophole was a way to rest in bed and claimed the same, all of us "heathens" had to toothbrush-clean M-16s with the meanest little drill sergeant instead.

One Sunday, Young Woman Me decided to take the troop bus to an evangelical church near base, treat it as a field trip. Maybe, she thought, she'd accidentally reconnect with a belief in grand goodness, see some speck of holistic holiness again through new custom. There, at the service, she took off her cap and learned all about the submissive roles women were supposed to play in a proper Christian community.

Apparently, the male preacher told us, we represent the softer side of God.

I replaced my BDU cap and boarded the bus back to my M-16. In the barracks upon arrival, I observed three women threaten to beat each other up for moving each other's laundry from the washers to the dryers without permission. And I wondered, as I had begun to wonder intermittently between childhood and adulthood, who had done the translating of God's wise words onto papyrus and paper for us. Because he seemed like a shitty secretary. Or else we couldn't read.

―

The myriad of jobs began in adulthood: for some of us, blue-collar trudging for blue-plate specials. Sinning on Saturdays: booze, more easily than prayer, eases aching joints. Then repenting on Sundays.

Some of us interned en route to rising in rank: the ad men, finance finessers, real estate mavens, skirting the evil edge of riches by donating, now and then, to church coffers.

Some of us, myself included (as mentioned), enlisted, despite early Christian theologian Tertullian's claims that the taking of human life should prevent Christians from participating in war, and despite Thomas Aquinas's assertion that war was always sinful, even if employed for "just" ends.

When I got to college eventually afterward and read this, I started to think differently about my brave Saint Joan.

Had she only been sainted because, after warmongering, she paid publicly for her violence on a hellish pyre?

I also began to wonder about the pieces of theology our teachers had selected, from the millions available, to teach us.

"Lapsed Catholic" is the joke, rolling pleasurably off the tongue in a kind of alliterative mini-poem, emotion packed in but leaking around the rhythmic edges of the phrase.

Every one of us who's "lapsed" has a story about it, typically tedious with disappointment. Maybe, whether you still attend Mass or not, you remember these moments:

When you saw Gospel readings regurgitated year after droning liturgical year, with no discussion after, just a lecture.

When it occurred to you that "Exaltation" wasn't actually joyful: so many ceremonies deployed with dutiful solemnity.

When you realized, encountering the larger sample size of the global world, that many people aren't Catholic, or even Christian, and that people of other faiths live life just fine too—and in fact are often *nicer* than your own spiritual brethren.

And, of course, when you realized that all Catholics are, in one way or another, Cafeteria Catholics themselves: advocating particular biblical quotes they like and quietly disregarding the rest.

In light of this disenchantment, over time, maybe your more mystical musings faded, as did mine.

When God was somehow socially aligned with guns, military might, military-mimicking competitive sports fervor, or all the red meat you could stuff yourself with stuffed onto a Ford-truck-sized Fourth of July BBQ grill, He appealed to me far less than Joan of Arc riding into battle on horseback: scrappy underdog, willing not just to *kill* but to *die* for the kindness of Christ (and France?). However hypocritical this, in itself, may also have been.

Gandhi did more in these last past decades, Adult Me started to think, than did the Jesus freaks, for social justice: and he was jailed.

MLK was murdered.

The Peace Pilgrim was killed in a car after walking 25,000 miles, seven times across the country, preaching peace.

None of them were canonized.

The Quaker banner in my new neighborhood read "There is no way to peace. Peace is the Way," promoting habit and discipline around the cause of empathy: not fancy ritual meant to signal virtue.

When I learned how white supremacists, over centuries, fused together the biblical stories of Ham (his Curse) and Cain (his Mark) into a formula they conveniently claimed "justified" contemporary racism, and coupled that with Adult Me's new college knowledge that with hundreds of biblical translations, parts were added, rephrased, replaced, and removed each century by people in power, my faith slid away entirely.

Adult Me went to church one more time, with her boyfriend's Irish grandmother on a bleak rainy day.

For a few moments the incense and holy water soothed; the familiar symbols, actions, and smells reminded her of Little Me's naïve and simple love of kindness.

But then the equation changed: Gospels were repeated, and the priest preached obedience, and very few of those words now squared with her ideas of rightness. Meaning was forged more actively and meaningfully where she existed now, in cities full of people that parts of the Bible said were bad: more in margins, among misfits where gayboys were sweet, than the cruel and careless gun-toting men of her youth, who were tasked at church to treat their fellow humans, *including their enemies*, better, but didn't. Plaid Pantry sold the same communion wine they had at St. Anne's up the street for $4.75, and she could give the spare change, instead of to the church's offering plate, directly to the beggar at the door.

After this slow slide from grace, the usual Rolodex of twenty-something tricks to orient a new worldview failed. Parents, peers, teachers, and friends all had advice about how to look at life, as did lovers, counselors, and people Adult Me met at parties. But how to really replace a preexisting "rightness" structure when it has collapsed entirely in on itself like a once-hopeful soufflé? There's a lot of data available. Lots of rumor. No one good answer.

So she tried all the advice, adding new "cards" to her "coping mechanism" mental files.

Maybe, like her, you bought a new car, changed jobs, or sought scaffolding in the arms of new lovers.

The novel activities of unfamiliar friend groups and attempted hobbies tempted as potential new replacement formulas to shape direction easily. The list lengthened to a litany: full-time work, part-time work, semi-committed college attendance, reading, drinking, dancing, hiking, biking, cooking, swimming, jogging, parties, meetings, and laughable attempts to meditate.

Nothing stuck.

My mom, witness to this rut roller-coaster of Young Woman Me, one day gave me an airfare coupon she'd gotten, randomly, in the mail. "See the world," she said. "Go for cheap. Get perspective."

So I put my finger on the price bubble of the cheapest location the ad coupon offered, which was London, and flew there alone. I marveled at the architecture as we descended, not minding that I then barfed up my first English pint near my hostel and my first spicy street curry too. When I got a handle on my nerves, I went touring, by myself alone for the first time, to museums without coercion from school trips.

At the Tower of London, the giant Queen's Ravens poked around the grounds cackling, and I was charmed until I learned their wings were clipped to keep them in Her Majesty's "service."

The weaponry inside astounded: broadswords and pikes by the hundreds, spiked balls on long rods and Spanish Morningstars lining the walls for room upon room, standing taller than two Henry-the-Eighth suits-of-armor stacked high. An army of armor, family crests, and gemstones amassed there all insisted on England's power: her moral righteousness in alignment with Providence. I photographed, in the British Museum, tiny medieval church chairs only suitable now for child-sized butts, the myriad portraits of squishy-looking royals, and pasty baby Christs and Marys. Each new aisle had an era: a wing, it seemed, for each continent that England, in her wisdom, had been kind enough to colonize, civilize, convert, and collect from.

It was only at the Tate, the last museum I visited, that I felt finally at ease: people painted in hundreds of varied new ways. Sometimes realistic and sometimes strange, they might be hyperbolically beautiful, lifelike, or mimicking malformation, with bunchy browbones or triangle faces. Some were shown as poor, like most of us are. Skins were a spectrum of hues. Cities were not uniformly slathered in sunlight, nor was Jesus clean and serene at his end.

The artists here, it seemed to me, had unique ways of receiving and then refracting the worlds in which they found themselves. I felt the usefulness of this variety in my expanding understanding.

After I tired of England's greatness, I took a train north, to wilder Scotland, on the recommendation of a fellow random pub patron. William Wallace, my mom's mom had told me, is an ancestor, and so: Why not? See our birthplace. Try on our tartan. Eat haggis.

In Scotland, where eons past, I'd heard, our ancestors were purged of their pagan practices by good Christians, the train chugged into Edinburgh station, and sound grew quieter.

I humped my little backpack along through spiky church spires and strange little underground streets.

I found places where nature met myth, and metamorphosed: Selkies shedding sealskins and kelpies keeping hooves when transmuting to human form. Giant eels, body snatchers, fairy creatures . . . what was real? My favorite pub commemorated Deacon Brodie, respected craftsman turned burglar, later transformed into Robert Louis Stevenson's Doctor Jekyll (and Mr. Hyde). Hume questioned the nature of truth: I saw his tomb.

I had some haggis.

I read some pamphlets about Nessie, the Loch Ness Monster, and arranged a trip to meet, if not her, at least her lake.

As evening fell, I found room at an inn and heard a "trad" band in the bar below toot on traditional pipes and pound ancient drums. The locals let me into their chatting: were curious, asked of my American dream, told me tales from their history. Their jokes were irreverent; their thirst to learn, slakeless.

Further from humanity, on a long trek into the Highlands, I let my eyes pass over bunchy rolls of earth, piled high into wrinkles in deep-rifted valleys, ancient brain shapes, a red hairy cow tucked here or there, while others rose rocky and dark: slate below their caps or capes of snow.

When I returned to my room, I gazed through lace curtains framing snowflakes and light from outside, held my hand high: it was dark, backlit and featureless, just a template for human form, and I thought it possible to see spirit in there.

What if I should have been a nun, as Little Me had wanted, alone in my cell but for this feeling; quiet communion? And what kind of life is possible, I wondered, when people let themselves revise rules that others have made?

When I came stateside again, Adult Me returned to her college endeavors, renewed.

In a kind of spiritual quilting, she began to sort through and seek out patchwork pieces of other's perspectives she liked and add them to her own, rather than struggling to swallow any one whole entirely.

In Asian studies classes, she warmed to Taoism: a credo of change, argument for adaptation.

In psychology, she craved cognition—forays into how we comprehend—and behavioral studies: needs, rewards, motivations.

She nerded out on nihilism and Gnosticism, enjoying, fully, the odd human ability to hold contradicting ideas as potentially true together.

Science fiction inspired with its social metaphor, and sociology provided ways to notice ideologies, then the deviations from them, through history.

She began to draw diagrams, maps, renderings of reality she saw or wished for: a bubbling blanket model of culture growth. Nongendered English. An adjusted Maslow's pyramid, with self-actualization and fulfillment near the middle instead of the end.
She fastened to the idea that one person could be uniquely themself and like everyone else simultaneously: apart, and part of a whole . . . or of a hole, depending on their state of mind.
She turned these notions, dissected, into school assignments, and when she came home, she still thought about them. Instead of witnessing a world in which conflicting values clashed confusingly, she could see it was possible to align them, and treat her time in her life as an adventure in trial-and-error puzzling, reliable learning.
Creativity can be a kind of faith.
What isn't yet real, in life, can be made so through the realm of the mind.
You can show your reality to others, in lieu of telling them what theirs should be.

After some years passed, I rediscovered some of you, old classmates, online.
We laughed about being Cafeteria Catholics.
Most of us stopped using this calculus, and some of you've dabbled, like me, in other maths: divine ratios, statistics, quantum foam.
We've toyed with horoscopes and enneagrams.
We've forgotten, it seems, old grievances, fears, and obedience.

Maybe there is no single guidebook or trail marker, after all.
Divinity shapeshifts, like Lazarus, and like ourselves.

And maybe communion with it is still sacred, but rather than being baked into a wafer, It simply exists, waiting potential energy, to be animated, then reanimated.

We mimic the act of creation, make God in our own images.

Review, renew, and revise, find new through-lines to the divine.

Transubstantiate.

One day, some years after my first trip to Scotland, I returned, student-work visa in hand and ready to stay for the summer in this place wherein I'd rediscovered largeness.

I got a job as a traveling salesgirl, selling imports around the Highlands with a group.

We'd drive to tiny towns out in the wilds, find the community hall, unroll our carpets, and set out our singing bowls.

We'd try to tell the locals how to rub their sides to make them sound: that these gold half-orbs were meant for spirit, not for porridge.

We encountered some skepticism.

Then one day, as we drove between towns, a huge loitering sheep with a spray-painted dot on its butt turned last-second to trot out in front of our Sprinter van, and we hit it. The driver, a kind New Zealander, rushed her hands to her cheeks and cried out, hating to have hurt it. Or worse.

Now what should we do? We'd have to find the farmer. Which farmer owned all the pink-spotted sheep, in this wide shared range of land?

Suddenly, as we opened the doors to approach our massacre, the sheep rose, like Lazarus. Though we'd struck it going thirty miles per hour, it just baaed in a pissed-off way, shook itself, and trotted away.

It had been only temporarily dead: its motion only ever paused.

Hol(e)y (II)

Portland, Oregon, in the early aughts, is divided into five major sections. Four quadrants: Northeast, Southeast, Northwest, Southwest. North and South are divided by Burnside Street. East and West are divided by the Willamette River, where a bunch of bridges arc across the sky in unique shapes and colors, representing different eras and modes of design. Above all that is the cap, NoPo (North Portland), where perhaps a person of lesser means could still buy a house. Everything is gentrifying: new buildings and businesses are rising from the rubble of the old ones coming down, and entire neighborhoods are undergoing overhaul. Since LP has lived there, she's seen a crush of yuppies come in from California, and hipsters hailing from Brooklyn, Chicago, Baltimore, Pittsburgh, everywhere. It is a city blind and blooming, as full of paradoxes as it is of parks: Forest Park, larger and wilder than most public spaces, is also home to not a small portion of Portland's rather huge homeless population. Locals like to brag that there are more strip clubs per square mile than in any other U.S. city, but also more churches. And "underemployment" is an overused word for the young arty "elite," but they do still manage to buy their drugs and booze and expensive, over-flavored coffee drinks, which everyone there seems to drink a lot of: booze and coffee both. They need it to participate: move quickly through oft-pelting raindrops, then relax and stroll coolly through the same slushy streets once it slows, the highs and the lows.

Like everyone else her age, LP works in food service. No, she works at Blockbuster. No, it's an allergy clinic. LP has fallen out of the expected script for a twenty-something having a "good time" as she goes to work each day on her cruiser bike, as she holds down little kids for blood draws and tries to avoid conversations with her coworkers, who enjoy grandchildren, homemaking, fad diets, and Jesus. She's had some trauma recently, having left the army ungracefully, so when she goes home from work, she tries to work it out: paints on plywood with housepaint that she buys on special from Home Depot's "mismatched" color table. She goes hiking with her boyfriend, Niles. They go out for beer at the Horse Brass with their friends: Cal (the drug dealer), Dante (the poet), Lawrence (the jerk), Gavin (the farm boy), Charles (the old man in a young body), Mina (a gardener), and sometimes Crazy Pat. Lawrence isn't actually her friend.

Crazy Pat, maybe not really crazy but a visionary, is a short, round, Germanic-looking musician who got into a lot of trouble in high school and consequently beats himself up for his lack of present-day success. Crazy Pat says when God created the world, he was shaking his head to the rhythm of a tambourine beat, then his head fell apart and tumbled into thousands of people all over the earth. LP thinks this is a beautiful creation story, and likes it much better than being a biblical outgrowth of a rib.

LP walks from Crazy Pat's apartment downtown by Portland State University to her own house. She tries to walk a lot, because the winter weather gets her down if she doesn't. She's restless. If she walks, she'll think less about going back to the office the next day.

Still, she goes back to the office the next day, where the building is square and drab and gray. She rides a slow elevator up three floors. As she watches the light behind the numbers on the wall panel move up, she hopes it will get stuck and she'll have to stay in the elevator all day instead of going to work, but it never happens. She walks down the hall, ducks into the restroom to straighten her hair, then walks to door 310 and opens it.

When she gets home, she lies down on the bed. The kitties come in and climb on her, meowing. They start to fight: Reginald H. Kittycat Esquire bites Penelope Thumper Pumpkinhead on the pumpkinhead, and so Penelope curls into a ball to kick him with her two back legs.

"Stop it, stop it." LP pulls them apart and puts them in different rooms like she would children, and they meow at each other across the house.

She smokes some weed, realizes the little tin in which they keep the house weed stash is nearly empty, and makes a note to have Niles call Cal. She zombies to the kitchen, makes cocoa, looks at the empty Crock-Pot everyone at work told her to buy, then goes back into the living room to sit on the couch in front of the half-painted hunk of plywood leaning on the wall. She puts the cocoa down, opens a can of cheap mis-tinted housepaint, makes one bright orange smear with a pinkened brush, knows it's all wrong, and goes back to lie on the bed some more.

When Niles gets home, he and LP decide to go for drinks and dinner, since both feel apathetic toward cooking. They put the cats in the one room without any houseplants and meet Charles at the Horse Brass. They all order fish-and-chips. The fish-and-chips arrive slightly burnt. Then Gavin comes in in his usual flannel shirt and talks about working on the Gremlin parked in the middle of his cow field. They poke fun at Charles for his too-bright Hawaiian shirt. They get a dart set from the bar and start to play. Crazy Pat arrives, then Mina, who gives everyone hugs, lights up the room with her enthusiasm, and demonstrates belly dancing moves, drawing the alphabet with her chest before sitting down. Lawrence enters and jokes about swinging cats around in a pillowcase. LP grunts and goes to the bathroom. As she emerges from the hallway where the bathrooms are, she sees her table full of friends from afar: throwing darts, ordering pints, chatting roundly, growing up. She feels warm and fuzzy from joy (or the Black Cherry Stout?), as long as she doesn't look at Lawrence. Cal sits beside Charles and Dante, who is depressed, but drinking, and so is currently slapping the table with his palms, elucidating enthusiastically either the work of Hunter S. Thompson, the proper way to use a horsewhip on a lover, the chemical components of a hallucinogen LP has never heard of, the grammatical structure of Esperanto, or the importance of Zero Population Growth. On this point Dante and LP agree. They used to date once too, for a month. She broke up with him the day before Valentine's Day, because his depression was intractable, but he had already ordered her roses.

After eleven it's time to go home, because they all have obligations. Gavin must be at the machinist's at five, where he will put on plastic protective glasses and endeavor not to get his long flaxen tresses caught in the drill press. Charles will separate dead fish from their heads for the sushi bar and try to ignore the fact that many of them have two heads, or three sets of fins, or four eyes. Lawrence will sell cell phones. Dante will drive to the community college and edit paltry poetry. Mina will walk to the preschool and insert earthworms into urban gardens with kids. Niles will go to the board shop and wax snowboards. LP will go to the allergy clinic.

Before this happens, Niles and LP fall asleep snuggled up, with the cats stuffed between them. They listen to the sound of the rain on the roof, and LP wonders what Pat will do the next day, because he's the only one who can't hold down a regular job. She wonders if she might prefer to be like Pat.

She pushes through door 310 again in the morning. Mallory, sturdy and pleasant, calls from the front desk, "Good Mooooorning!"

"Hello," says LP on automatic. "How are you?"

"Very well." They smile, following their script, and LP turns down the hall to the kiddie section. She procures some hot tea from the spigot attached to the sink. She sits at her desk. She says hello when people come in. Pretty soon she is asked to process some blood samples. She goes to the lab room and squirts blots of blood from each test tube onto a microscope slide. She walks it over to the dry ice room, turns on the machine, waits for the sound to grow thick, then lifts the ice out with potholders and packs it with the sample. She stretches tape across the box, labels it, puts it outside in the courier case for pickup.

"Boy, we're really booked full tomorrow," says Eileen, back in the room across the hall.

LP nods and considers calling in sick.

But she doesn't, and on Friday after work she and Niles decide to celebrate the weekend by driving out to Cal's new place in Beaverton to meet with pals. Ordinarily no one would go to Beaverton for fun, but the group of friends have exhausted the pool halls and the bar scene along with their bar funds this month. There aren't any good films out, the weather is *shit*, and sitting home with a book, spanking the cats when they chew on the raggedy houseplants, sounds like misery on a stick.

At Cal's there's a snake in the bathtub. LP doesn't see it until she already has her pants around her ankles, prepped and ready to pee. When she comes squealing back suddenly from the bathroom, the roomful of guys are grinning.

"Hardy-har-har," she says. "Does it bite?"

"It might if you scare it," Cal tells her, "but it can't get out of the tub."

So LP goes back into the bathroom. She takes a seat and looks over. Quiet, a curious creature, the snake hovers in the bottom of the tub, tongue flicking in dashes of red.

Its scales, nearly seamless, seem wet, and LP wonders if she should touch it. Her hand aches for contact.

"Hi, snah-kay," she says. "You're not too bad, are ya? Long as you don't escah-pay."

After she pulls her pants up, she runs her hand across the smooth stretch of the creature, but only in her mind. In her mind, the snake licks her kindly, like a dog, and she feels calm. She leaves without flushing, so as not to bother it.

She goes out into the living room and sits down in Memoryville, while the boys mix drinks, talk rot, measure fingers of weed on a white medical scale on the table before her.

She remembers soaking with them in a hot tub, up in the West Hills, where all the rich folks lived, including someone's stepdad. How it overlooked everything, and the lights from below glimmered through the passing mist, and they felt like a little team of space cadets, a pod of people suspended above the rest of the city. They felt special, because they had each other, even if the rest of Portland was nuts. They shared some wine. They wet their necks and heads, and sat up out of the water into the chilly black air whenever they got too hot. That evening was the first night she and Niles kissed, after everyone else had gone to bed. She remembers how they grinned at each other and she was happy, because she knew she wouldn't have to split time between this lover and her friends. She was lucky, really, a very extraordinarily lucky person.

At the end of the night, Niles and LP say goodbye to Cal and the snake, then drive back into Portland to finish a weekend full of chores, dabbling in paint and kitties and parents and shopping, then getting ready for work again.

"Ah roo roo," says Niles.

"Ah roo roo roo," says LP, meaning, in dogspeak, "I love you too."

On Monday she drags back into work. Halfway through the day, she trades tea for coffee.

"Can you help with a blood draw?" says Eileen, poking her head around the corner.

"Of course," says LP. She joins them in the exam room, recognizes the child Hester, whose blood she'd helped steal before, and says, "Hi, Hester. Don't worry, it'll be easy this time."

Hester looks up at her from the paper-padded exam bed with big round eyes, and knows LP is lying. LP sets herself with elbows locked, one arm on Hester's right ankle, one arm on Hester's forearm. When Hester's screaming becomes thrashing, LP leans the weight of her body down across Hester's stomach and legs, pinning her in place.

"She's got those darned rolling veins," mutters Eileen, sweat starting to peak on her forehead.

When they're done, LP goes to the bathroom and looks into the mirror, Hester's face swimming there like liquid inside her eyes. She looks at her tired, pale face, hair straining to escape its ponytail, the conventional bead necklace above the Kmart collared office shirt, and thinks, something has to give.

She comes back out and has just settled down to some paperwork when Eileen pokes her head in again and says, "Line one's for you."

It's Niles.

"Come home," he says to LP.

Something bad has happened.

Crazy Pat and Dante speak of leaving. They were close friends with Cal, who's been killed. Pat goes to stay with Dante awhile. People worry.

But Pat helped his parents name his sister after a *Doctor Who* character, and he wants to go to Britain now to work on the new version of the show. After Cal's funeral, he puts together a demo tape of scores he thought could accompany each different scene: a rousing ditty for a chase, another for a monster, even some tinkling trip-hop tunes for the psychedelic time-travel. But no one returns his phone calls from the BBC. So he plans to go there in person. All he needs is five hundred bucks, he says. He becomes a vacuum salesman, cuts himself a 1970s vacuum salesman mustache, and goes to work.

Dante, meanwhile, decides to take a road trip. He still lives with his parents, trading laundry and dish duties for rent, and he has saved. Within the next six months he'll trade his rain jacket for T-shirt, gloom for adventure, executing a journey through most of the continental forty-eight states to read, write, learn, meet amazing new people, and figure out what to do with his life now that he no longer wishes to be a drug dealer. Now that he's trash-bagged a significant portion of the drug paraphernalia he kept in the lockbox below his bunk bed. Since he saw what happened to Cal, his dreams are haunted by the risk that profession entailed.

Gavin starts thinking he'll leave LaCenter, desert his pet scrap cars, and go to art school. Get his tall farmboy body moving in new ways that don't involve sweeping machine shops or cattle prodding.

They go on little road trips, Gavin, LP, Niles, and Mina: to Seattle, to the beach, to other out-of-the-way places all around the Northwest. It's soothing, calming, those tires against the road. Niles flips the dials on the radio, and LP imagines his translucent hair falling forward into his eyes the way it used to in high school, though he's taller now, with deeper eyes, and a hairline, receding, hidden always under a cap. Mina laughs almost like she used to, though her brown eyes go flat when she watches lumber trucks pass on the road.

Dante prepares diligently for his road trip. LP is hopeful for his mental health. Maybe now Dante can learn to be happy. He'll see sunlight and smile, even if Nietzsche was right and there is no God, and most people in the world are mean or dumb.

Since Dante's saving his pennies, he doesn't go with Niles and LP and Mina to Seattle to get drunk at ten different bars on Mina's twenty-first birthday, or cheer her on gallantly while she pukes out a poorly painted second-story window afterward. Dante drives up to Gavin's farm instead, to practice using his new gun, in case he needs to fend off road villains in the underbelly of our great wild nation. But then he gets a DUI on the way home from the farm.

LP talks with Crazy Pat about it later. Pat knew Dante was upset, but hadn't heard him leave at 4 a.m. to climb Mt. Tabor, same gun in tow, to vent his frustration about the little door of hope he'd envisioned now sliding shut. To startle the runner, who called the police to scrub the now pulpy, now red oak tree and surrounding grass patch clean before daylight. It would have been a nice place to go, at least: one can see the whole city from that fine vantage, the west-facing side of the east city walking loop. But LP worries Crazy Pat will be even crazier now.

They go to Little Chapel of the Chimes together, look down into the box. Dante is waxen. But otherwise the same.

Wake up, LP thinks, poking him with her presence. Wake Up.

"I don't know why they put him in a beanie," she complains.

Dante, laid out flat, looks like he's about to arise from a nap and go outside into winter, but has only remembered his hat.

After a moment Charles turns to her and says:

"Because the back of his head's not there."

LP has a dream the night before she leaves Portland. It is the dream of Cal's death. She watches the customer, tall, dark, perhaps handsome, push Cal into the bathroom. Into the tub. Use the knife.

Again.

Again.

The neighbors think he is singing. They eat TV dinners in the adjoining rooms while LP tries to call them for help.

But she can't. She stands frozen in the doorway while the snake hisses and strikes at the ankles of the men still struggling in the tub.

She wakes in a sweat, heartbeat sure as rain on her windowsill.

"They think we're singing, but we're screaming."

There's a poem about that somewhere.

She finds it on the internet.

Prints it out.

Tears it up.

Eventually she moves away. Gavin's gone to art school in Canada. Pat went to Britain and came back with no contract from the BBC. Charles, Niles, Mina, and Lawrence have all stayed around in Portland: Mina makes gardens, Charles tops trees, and Niles makes furniture. LP doesn't remember what happened to the snake. Was it in the bathtub, she wonders, the whole time Cal was dying? She finds herself wanting to adopt it, pet it, ask it about his final moments. But someone took the snake, or found a home for it. LP doesn't know what happened to Lawrence either, nor does she care.

When she visits, she finds some things have changed: Little Chapel of the Chimes has become a brew pub, where they could all go and eat fish-and-chips, but they never do. They go to other places, do new things, when they meet now. When they talk, they find metaphor, strange memory: hats attached to hearts, tongues to ankles, smiles to skulls and waiting tree bark. Many points of pressure seem to push them apart past themselves, and simultaneously suck them back together, like bullets shoved into motion, or a knife sliding deep past the skin: particles imprinted into cells, again and again.

So they live, and grow.

Remember to love.

"Ah roo roo."
"Ah roo roo roo."

Pulse

I put on a coat, kiss Mum goodbye, and step into the night.

From Mt. Tabor, next to Gramma's house, I can peer from forested darkness out to glittering city: a gently threadbare blanket of mostly amber lights.

It looks warmer over there to the west, energetic, from where I shiver here on this dim, littler lump of land.

So without thinking too much about it, but careful not to slip down my muddy, grassy shortcut, I trail down to the rain-slick street and then along the bus route in case I hear one coming, sneakers smacking nothing but cold, wet pavement.

During the day I go to school, and send faxes for attorneys on the sixteenth to nineteenth floors of a fancy corporate litigation firm downtown. But it's part-time. Broke and living again at Gramma's, though Gramma herself is gone, I seek something, though not sure what.

I can smell dampness, rotting moss, and oak as I go. In upper Hawthorne, wooden bungalows are lit by lampposts. In between the houses: dark, coniferous, spiked shadows. It's a quaint-West-Coast-comfy-money part of town. I can imagine the people inside have planks of Pacific salmon cooling on granite countertops, and curl into Pendleton wool blankets with tea to listen to NPR. This is not where I'm headed. I've been invited to go dancing with the young set of my law-firm colleagues for five bucks. The venue is the Fez, on West Burnside and about 20th, a mere seventy-ish blocks from here. When I reach the end of this neighborhood, I find myself deposited onto Hawthorne Street, still without a bus.

Hawthorne used to be a hippie haunt. Of course, it's transformed now into a hip shopping district for yuppies. I've viewed askance, for some years now, the upscale-edgy hair salon that replaced the mom-and-pop pizza shop, which usurped the previous no-pain piercing place, which shoved out the headshop where I could buy glass pot pipes in high school.

Since the usually reliable frequent-service bus shows no signs of showing up, and I need to keep warm, I keep walking: past the pool hall, the organic farmer's market, the sneaky little independent theater where I slipped in once and found an aerial dance troupe practicing. An Indian joint. A Chinese joint. An Italian joint called The Italian Joint. People still spill from these eateries despite the late evening hour, and I smile at them because they smile at me. I can see my breath hang in the air before each step I take along bus route 14. I train my eyes toward Grand, past the bars I am tempted now to enter. I wonder when Grand Avenue was grand. Arriving here, at the corner of the lonely Rose and Raindrop, still hanging on seemingly since the twenties and mostly empty despite its dark wood counters and gold burnished banisters, I look around: fast-food trash in the gutter, unhoused people crouched in doorways. Here, a couple, fighting, burst staggering from a stairwell. Another corner of Portland trying to be Grand, but coming up Drunk instead?

At Burnside, all but two thin lanes are closed for bridge construction, breeding an eerie calm. I find myself alone amidst a myriad of orange traffic cones. Water under the bridge, as I near, reflects an opaline black and emanates the sharp smell of cold. If I listen, I can hear small waves slap metal beams, but softly. In the middle of the bridge, overlooking and between two halves of the same city, a chill wind fills my lungs, spreads stray hair strands across my face, forces my eyes to tear up now with its sting.

I finally feel calm.

I suppose I could stand here for an hour or two, even settle down with my legs looped through the grate of the pedestrian fence. Or lean out over the rail and look. Maybe I should.

My legs tingle. My mind is clear. But I've promised to be at another somewhere sometime soon, so this moment must fold up and fizzle.

I pass the big Oregon-shaped sign, neon-lit, into downtown. I pass bars and card rooms, more people in their boxes, preparing for sleep. There's the place with the motorcycles hung from the ceiling, and the bench outside where I made out with a paralegal, who complimented my free spirit and then went back to his ex. I gaze up the street I normally take to go to the cubelike law firm, although usually I'm on a bus, and then I keep walking. I'll be there inside the cube again soon.

When I reach the Fez, my calves are screaming. I pay my five bucks and limp up the long wooden stairwell squeezed in next to the drifter hotel next door.

Purple plush curtains spread wide to reveal a large well-kept room: tall windows, distant ceilings. A spray of handsome folks scatter on the dance floor.

"Hey!" and there's my coworker, waiting to introduce me to her friend.

"This is Jay."

We shake. Jay is nice. One day, Jay will go on to be in a band, which will be famous. I'll hear their songs while shopping for socks in a Target. But tonight, he's just Jay and he's nice.

I order a purple cocktail, and then the group of people around us grows larger. The talking is too loud to hear any of the talking. I meet a towhead with good tattoos. I meet a tall, thin, quiet man. Our redheaded file clerk appears, and one of the younger lawyers. A girl with good cheekbones swirls her floral-print skirt around her thighs, and pretty soon we're all, instead of talking, spinning: butts and hips and gaping grins. Twisting torsos. Little sins: fingers slipped through belt loops, a tongue tucked into the ridge of an ear, two teeth surrounding the naked nape of a neck. Collarbones collide. The motion occurs at shutter speed.

Between the blinking and bleating and corresponding bass thuds, I notice that the thin man, the tallest center of the crowd around which we all have begun to revolve, has slipped his shy demeanor. He shatters himself on the dance floor, head heavenward, eyes tight, mouth frozen in a wince of ecstatic strain, every other part of him moving like a knife. Precisely, he leaps up and mimics the shooting of a gun, expanding himself toward the ceiling. Then he lands down on both knees—I swear I hear them crack—arms stretched out wide and then cradling what at first I think is a faux child, then understand when his fingers walk, ascending: an air guitar. Which I learn later he does for part of his living.

"Well, he doesn't like to be tied down," my coworker says when I ask for his number two days later.

"Neither do I," I reply, and she jots it down for me. I pocket the scrap and go send some faxes. I wheel a creaky metal mail cart around each gray-carpeted sixteenth-floor corner, briefly confusing two like-named attorneys, then roll around the other floors, dropping each letter or legal brief into a uniformly stained-wood desktop in-box. By three, I'm making copies of archdiocesan files: someone's defending pedophilic priests.

Thin Man, I heard, went to my Catholic high school, though I didn't know him then.

There's my coworker who went back to his ex-girlfriend: we wave hi in the hall.

I have some lunch, then make coffee for meetings.

Later, at home, I nap, and have nightmares about dropping the archdiocesan copy project out of its stacked five-inch binders by mistake.

I wake and call Thin Man. He sounds surprised to hear from me, but does remember meeting.

"Sure," he says when I ask if he'd like to get a beer, "that sounds nice."

Then, "What are you doing tonight?"

We meet on East Burnside, at a poshy burger bar. The walls are lined in great circles of wood, slices of tree trunks all enameled together. The bathrooms are flashing mirror-mosaics. The bar music barely covers the sound of the concert in the basement, and noisy hotel guests splash, squealing, in the adjoining building's late-night pool.

We greet with a hug, the standard Portland trustbuilder, despite not knowing one another very well.

His touch is polite.

We order beer and beef.

As I stare at his eyebrows, long, dark, and framing deep-set eyes, he asks how my day was: instantly intimate. I stammer. Blather on about the law firm.

I tell him I won't be there forever.

Big plans.

He tells me relatable stories of motion. He seems to like it too.

Like me, he's walked all night.

Quit jobs on the spot.

Left lovers.

Like me, he seems to be sifting through the world for some other way to be.

He once biked the whole California coast alone, eating only hard-boiled eggs.

When he bailed out of New York after a breakup, he came home, here, to Portland. But he still has trouble sleeping, even away from famed NYC speed.

I tell him how, younger, I climbed from my upstairs window for love.

"What happened to the boyfriend?" he asks.

"That was high school." But I blush.

"When's the last time you had your heart broken?" he asks.

It feels like we're getting undressed.

At 4 a.m. he rides me home on the back of his bike, wheels slicing sleek blacktop past my dangling legs and shoes. The streets are still snot-slick, and we ride them home from the bar, all forty-odd blocks back to my house, a slow go uphill. I see quiet streets as we pass: darkened buildings, dawdling drinkers, and those trying to sleep now on concrete.

We come to my grandma's house, and he parks in front of the roses.

I invite Thin Man into my basement room, show him my books. He describes his favorite, Henry Miller, a wanderer, who thought women must have harmonicas hidden up inside themselves, for how eagerly men seem to pursue them.

I tell him Hemingway's my current favorite: wanderer, war writer.

He asks me why.

He finds it fascinating, like they all do, that I went AWOL once.

"I thought about joining the military," he says. "They told me I could be a drummer boy."

"They tell you lots of things," I say.

"Do you still have nightmares?" he asks when I've told the whole tale.

"About being caught?" I unwrap myself from the damp wool things I've worn against the wind.

He nods.

"Sometimes," I say, "if I sleep."

My bed is tucked between a furnace, a bookshelf, and a crumbling basement wall.

"I'm sorry it's so small," I say, when we tangle into the wall.

"I'm not," he says.

His legs are long, and they don't fit onto the mattress, so he curls them around me.

In the darkness, I can feel his joints, the little hairs on his limbs.

Eyelids, long and soft. Eyebrows, thick. Without the light, I discover that his shoulder blades are as delicate as bird bones. I turn and press into the gaps between us. His hands feel nice in my hair.

After a bit, we sleep.

Later that week he and Jude, his friend with good tattoos, bake me a pie: blueberry.

I'm charmed, and we make beach plans.

We three leave town that weekend when Thin Man gets off a late wait shift. It's midnight when we come through the coast range, mountains so dense and damp you feel Bigfoot waiting to embrace you.

Pacific City, its own giant seastone mimicking the farther north and photo-famous Haystack Rock, emerges, inky.

A few scattered stars and an amber moon diffuse through whisped clouds to light the dunes, clumped together, yellow.

Thin Man leaves to pee, and I sit down with Jude on a sandbar, watch an iridescent tributary feed away into darkness.

The seafoam thuds, sparkling, onto sand like a body exhausted.

I rearrange my legs where we sit, and look out into that expanse: immersion, engulfment, the lunar weight pushing and pulling the current through and past itself.

Jude and I chat, but after a while we hear a new sound. Scratching, distant, stop-start. It sounds like an insect, maybe nearing, but eventually not.

"What *is* that?" I ask.

"Sounds like an animal?" Jude asks.

I stub out my cigarette.

"Should we go see?" I say, sharply aware we've lost Thin Man.

We stand up and crouch, waves thumping like a rhythmic record's end. The sense of supernatural is strong as we draw in upon the scratching.

Through that tallest clump of snake grass, the sound comes closer, but it makes no sense: not one-directional, but constantly changing, then changing again, not quite repeating.

"It's an alien!" I whisper. I always wanted a math chip in my mind, and I joke: maybe I can get my implant!

But I'm also unnerved. I'm not really sure I want to see behind the snake grass.

"One, two, three!" we say, and we peek.

There, in the moonlight, Thin Man slides.

Pirouettes.

Glides.

Like on a skating rink.

Then he lifts and replaces each leg, and tiny sea shrimp pop like sparks into the air where he steps with muddy tennies. I watch the skinny legs tango between small white stones, dancing in a seeming field of eggs without crushing any of them.

Turn.

Scritch.

Turn.

In the moonlight, his face pales where wrinkles trap photons. The tips of his fingers trace darkness as they fling left and right, into shadow, into vision, back to shadow again.

"Wow," I breathe reverently, giving myself away. Jude looks at me, smiles awkwardly.

I take in air, not tired anymore. I walk a few paces up, then stand still.

The earth is most alive before it crumbles. Is that what I've been told? And is that what I'm feeling? An earthquake beginning? Trepidation about the state of my blood, tumbling through me too quickly, makes me wake, suddenly, electric.

A week or two later, the earth has rotated and tides have shifted.

In the wake of thundering beach foam, flailing remnants of passion remain, tattered tidbits now, in the sand.

Thin Man and I have a boring brunch, where I find I've become too awestruck to say anything of interest. Our conversations start and stop like train cars unhinged, bumping into one another on the track.

I ask him, boringly, about his band. He says something unmemorable, then talks about his job. He makes fun of someone or other. I tell him I might change colleges again. He scoffs at school, and though I don't like making fun of school or other people, I do still follow him around for a month. I show up at his shows. His music is loud. He screams instead of singing. In his sexy suit, he talks to everyone around, but to me gives just a curt "hi." He's human, it turns out: as moody and daytime dull as the rest of us.

The last time I see him, he's come to my party, three months or so later: my last hurrah. Before my grandma's house will be sold, and my mom will move, and I will leave the state again, my friends and I fill her house with art. Jay's band, who I met when I met Thin Man, play in the basement. Thin Man is there for ten minutes, says "Whee" as he passes me on the stairs, then leaves. My old friends, the handful from high school I love, help me clean in the morning. We cart Gavin to the hospital after an art deinstallation accident.

Their care, in Thin Man's absence, feels abundant.

―――

The following week, my last in the city, I walk the streets alone. Maybe I think I'll run into Thin Man, or some other old love, or I'm simply saying farewell to the space.

Whatever the case, I ponder my leaving. I could live here in Portland: I have people. There's new artistic action and traction. So what's so wrong about staying?

But the law firm has offered to cocoon me in a permanent paralegal position, and it could keep me tied up here for years.

Besides, though I'm loved by my family, and various other fond folks for miles, whether I love myself is still a question.

The carnival looks different tonight.

On Burnside, people scatter, supine. One sad soul is laid long in a doorway upon an unfurled sleeping bag—the most traditional pose. Another is wrapped completely in a blanket, sticking legs-out from a box. I pass two more people curled together in a ball, against a wall, then the wild-eyed man who used to beg at my high school Subway shop, awake and still shaking his coin cup.

I can't help thinking they're me.

Could I wander too long, reject and refuse to live inside the common spaces of the world until, someday, maybe I couldn't?

What if I never have a law-firm salary?

Or any reliable salary ever?

I give myself an experiment. I won't use my bank cards tonight. Since I really rely on credit or debit, which requires jobs, jobs that require home addresses and showers and mental health, let me see how it feels to strip down my safety.

Step 1: I'm hungry.

At the 7-11 on Stark, they sell jerky medallions for twenty-five cents out of a plastic reach-in tub. I buy four with four quarters. That will be dinner.

Step 2: I'm rather wistful. But with only cash, I can't afford a fifteen-dollar cocktail, casual company, and a tip. So I buy a beer from the cooler: dessert and creature comfort at once.

I decide to keep walking with my beer. The houses somehow seem colder, darker tonight, but maybe it's because I see them as potential resting places should I get tired. The buses will stop running, and I don't have cab fare home, and legs eventually do get tired. If a cop sees me walking with my beer, it won't be good, but I care about it less as I drink.

The side streets are whisper quiet: just raindrops here. So I swerve closer back toward Burnside, where there's light and people close enough to hear me if I scream, but I could still sink down and sleep without a hassle.

I'm a fully housed, employed young person with plans, and I still feel a creeping at each corner. I imagine, as my muscles stiffen, what paranoia passes through a strained, at-risk body.

I pass a swath of buildings with people at their bases, none of them scheduled for massages this week, colon cleanses, the self-care packages advertised farther up the street.

Nobody buying down comforters here or grousing about a heat bill.

Here, human faces are concealed—with grime, worry, errant hair, anger.

The most ominous shape is upcoming: a diminutive person in a wheelchair, slumped down deep into the seat of it, blue tarp thrown over their head. I initially think there's not even a person there, or that the person could be decapitated. I get closer, though, and I can see their neck, intact but cracked sideways into a shoulder, barely visible. I imagine an already contorted spine sending nervous impulses up and down, frantically: Stop! Sit up straight! And I marvel: By what method is such an impulse ignored? The bottle? The needle? Total exhaustion?

I wonder how the wheelchair owner can be sure their chair won't roll away if someone decides to be mean and kick the stopper up.

But I doubt they have a choice whether to be here, like I do.

Across the street in the public park, on the concrete floor of a covered public patio, I slump, legs outstretched, listening to street sounds.

Is it like this to wander forever, where only your body is your home?

I curl into my jacket for warmth, though my beer has long gone, and with it all numbness.

Then I tell myself to walk, but anywhere seems far.

So I'll try to sleep, I think.

After an hour or so, though, my tailbone aches terribly.

My feet sweat inside soggy shoes.

When I do manage to drift off, a slow scraping awakens me.

A hunched, gray-haired man makes his meandering way past me in a pair of heavy, worn boots. He lifts a bundle I hadn't noticed from the shadows, and I can just make out the writing on its side, inked onto foam in black Sharpie: "Bob's Bed."

I realize I've displaced him. Maybe he's used to it, but still.

The skills of the restless, I realize, are the opposite of ours:

Keep possessions close, and small, just what you fit on your back.

Eat your food fast, for you've no place to save it.

Spend your money now, or someone else will.

Sleep, or keep moving: only this moment matters.

I shudder, feeling bad about Bob's bed space.

I decide that I don't really want frostbite.

I opt to get up and go home.

Tonight, time can stretch away to tendrils, but more than this moment should matter. There will be more, and tomorrow I should think about the rest: what happens next.

Mend motion with stability somehow.

Try to make more than spare change.

Drive (II)

On Greyhound again, some years later and southbound, the wiry young guy seated next to me intimidated. His hair hung shaggy in spikes under his baseball cap, which read "Depot Bay." He'd twisted a giant black fishhook up through the brim.

When he caught me gawking, I asked nervously about the writing on the hat. "That's a beach town, isn't it?"

"I'm a fisherman!" he said, with great enthusiasm, pointing to the hook.

"College," I said, when he asked where I was going, and only summarized the details about it being, now, at twenty-four, my fourth attempt.

"I was a bad student too," he said.

I wanted to squeak that I was actually a good student, I was just having trouble finding the right stuff to learn. But he interrupted me to ask where.

"Arizona."

"That's a long haul!" he said. "From Oregon."

I knew it was, but it was cheap. So I'd change lines in L.A. and then shoot out eastward.

Somewhere south of Springfield we picked up more passengers. Then off through golden hills, rippling meadow grass, we hummed along. Some folks chatted. At the first Grant's Pass sign, a skinny red-bearded man rose from the back.

"My god," he said, "there it is!"

"You goin' home, man?" asked another.

The redhead began to cry and laugh all together. He'd been in prison fourteen years, he said. He'd beaten up a man, left him for dead. But the man had crawled back to safety, and to the cops.

Next to me, Depot Bay Man twisted around like his fishhook.

"Hey, man, if you're gonna kill someone," he said, "you gotta think it through."

Which, he explained, he had, and described the process: Make sure someone is dead, take them onto a boat, then push them through a wood chipper into the sea. Push the wood chipper into the sea afterward.

The little party chatting near the back nodded appreciatively. Many of them, I learned, had also done time.

"Good plan, man!"

"Never thought of that!"

They wished the redhead best of luck, and he hopped off into his future, while I pretended, palms sweaty, to sleep. When Fishhook asked, at a rest stop, for me to buy beer—"They'll never suspect you!"—I told him I had no ID.

"I seem to have lost it," I said, "somewhere along the way."

Erasure

The desert is an ocean that simply stopped rolling one day.
I'm tired, it said, and its fish lay down into dinosaurs.
Seaweed sprouted thorns.
White wave crests became summits.
Sea depths became canyons.
Clouds remained clouds.

You tell Tim that when you die, you want to be buried in a tree. Or put on a platform in a tree. It's okay if parts fall down after a while: whatever. The great desert scavenging birds can pick bits of you up and ferry them around the region—an eyeball for Prescott, a tongue for Tucson. You don't mind your body lying quietly *on* the ground, busily disintegrating, you just don't want it stuffed, tucked, or folded away *into* the ground. Some years ago now, you glimpsed the winter wall of cold wet earth behind your friend Feather's lowered casket and grimly wondered how long it would take him to be fully erased as Feather and reabsorbed into the rest of the world—soil, worms, plant roots. Then maybe reemerge? You and Tim discuss how caskets are built too elements-proof these days, meant to stop or delay this process of disintegration and, thus, subsequent reintegration.

"Which is why I want a wood box," he says. "A hundred dollars, tops."

When your grandma, born in 1914, was a farm girl in Eastern Oregon, those who died ended up in pine. While still living, they had no refrigeration for meat, so they just salted it to preserve it as best they could. They had no indoor bathroom for the passing of it, so they used an outhouse. In the winter, although Eastern Oregon is mostly desert, it freezes just like the prairies of Idaho and Wyoming and mountain-desert Flagstaff (where Feather rests), so Gramma didn't want to go outside to the bathroom and developed a mean case of hemorrhoids. You discovered this by way of your mom, who also had hemorrhoids, and surgery for them in her thirties, which removed the lowest six-inch portion of her bowel. Being of the same genetic stock, you yourself have been to the bum doctor at a younger-than-normal age. And this year, when the doctors found and sliced away A Suspicious Polyp (you named her Polly) from the squeaky clean depths of your prepped and vacated colon, you began to think about mortality: about shedding the shell of the large-nosed, working-class, youngish white woman you see in the mirror every day. You've put in your requests. "Next time around," you say to the quieter part of your mind that doubles as your sense of the divine, "I'd like a better singing voice and a bigger butt. If I become a future me, a silicon mental chip to make math equations easier. Or, just make me a cactus."

The desert, which is in Eastern Oregon but also Arizona where you've lived for the last ten years, is often spoken about as an isolated, harsh, and dangerous place. It's difficult for vegetation to burst forth in the same thick way it does in climates full of ready water, where the ground fairly bubbles with swaths of tree root, thatches of grass, and spongy moss. Lots of vegetation in the Arizona desert also has spines. Some of the most clever carnivorous birds hang their lizard prey on those spines for easy aerial eating, leaving skeletons, like men hanged at the entrance of an old medieval village, scattered throughout the mine-like fields of dirt and rock. The animals, spiked too, arm for battle naturally and perpetually with sharpness: fangs, claws, scales, and plates.

The farther you get into Arizona, into deepest desert, the more the land is stripped of clutter. It is a place where the banalities and contradictions of the human world become more obvious. Between Phoenix and Tucson, off the I-10, the Florence penitentiary looms from the sand, and road signs warn against picking up hitchhikers. Farther south, the border: tent cities, cages. Up north, abandoned pueblos and mines. Scattered throughout the great vistas between: resource-scarce reservations (a different kind of prison), meth houses (a different kind of prison), megachurches (arguably yet another kind of prison). Indeed, says the desert, you humans are just as cruel as us, let's be frank about it. The visual elemental attributes of the desert may lead some to view it as particularly brutal compared to other places, but in a way the brutality breeds relief: it only takes two days to thirst to death, a half day of sunstroke to cook, or an hour to be eaten by a mountain lion—a place free of bullshit and distraction, falsity.

Someday, after human beings have done their worst to the global ecosystem, the world will fall plainly into its extremes, anyway: ocean and desert with little between. When you go to Wupatki, the gently sloping vacated ruins outside Flagstaff, you can still see trilobites curled and now stationary, imprinted into orange rock. The desert is an ocean that simply stopped rolling one day. I'm tired, it said, and its fish lay down into dinosaurs.

When the sliding doors at the Phoenix Sky Harbor International Airport spat you out into its roasting-kiss, tough-love heat for the very first time, off the plane from Oregon, you didn't know your husband Tim yet, but you encountered the 115-degree dry air he grew up in immediately. It rose upward in semi-pleated, visible waves from the pavement, and your breath was sucked out from your lungs to meet it without your permission. When you commented on this breathless sensation to a baggage porter, he nodded, "Yup," and mentioned that the airport even grounds planes when the air gets too hot and too thin.

Then you clambered onto the little northbound shuttle and it rose, perhaps like a phoenix, from the strip malls and fast-moving freeway traffic into steep brown hills dotted with little greenish shrubs. Later you would come to appreciate Phoenix—its luminescent pink streetlights pearling in small globes on the surfaces of silver skyscrapers in the plane-streaked night sky—but on this, the first desert day, you were glad to retreat. As your shuttle climbed into the very base of the Bradshaw Mountains, spindly palo verde and iconic arms-up saguaro, thousands of them, as far as your myopic eyes could strain to see, stood in stark contrast to Oregon's massive pine trees. You had many avid hiker friends in the Pacific Northwest, and while you too could appreciate the seeping smell of moss and the mystery of the thick fog that clings deep in the hill crevices of your birthplace, you'd told those same friends you felt corralled by the darkness; you'd gotten claustrophobic amidst the histories of heroin, grunge music, *Twin Peaks* imaginings, and the actual serial killers, who seem partially seeded by a Seasonal Affective Disorder that seeps late into spring and early summer. A zen koan torn from a daily meditation mini-book and long pinned to your wall had questioned, "What is the shape of my life?" then answered with another question, "What is the sound of rain?" Well, after life in Portland yielded one seeming emotional dead-end after another, you'd grown tired of trying to decipher the sound of rain. You were ready with the sunscreen, ready with binoculars, for heat, for light. You pressed your cheek now to the window of the shuttle, wide-eyed, ready for vast expanse, enormous like space must be to an astronaut standing at the door of the spaceship, waiting to see if she can breathe at the threshold.

Prescott, pronounced "Press Kit" or "Preskett" by locals, was where you found yourself. Your online horoscope location chart, in which you have about 12.6 percent confidence, lists this latitude as a place that will "render a pleasant environment for someone with your birth lines," and apparently it has been pleasant, too, for a lot of other pseudo-science hippie types before you. They came in droves in the 1960s and 1970s to sit in vortexes, supposed thin spots in the physical/metaphysical veil.

They communed with the spirits, bought up a lot of prime real estate, and opened rock and tarot reading stands, souvenir shops showcasing pioneer and native history.

Generations before that, other birth lines, your ancestors, your pioneering grandma's grandmas, clopped overland vaguely westward from the East. Like them, you would have a lucky freedom of motion, a kind of mobility dampened, after their arrival, for native residents of the region. Your language was readily spoken here now, your culture easily available. Your education, while incomplete and tenuously funded, had gotten you this far. You had a chance, and you felt grateful for it: to try college again at a tiny school up in the hills, leaning toward liberal arts and global social justice, which included the environmental aspects of that. You didn't come here to buy or to sell, to colonize or to convert, but you suppose, in a way, you came to commune. Something inside you said to come and listen, that maybe the environment and the arts and social justice were actually connected entities, enmeshed in ways you, firmly installed in modernity, didn't know yet and hadn't considered. You had an instinct that some of the barriers of your past were more permeable than you were taught: that in other times and places, instead of being a three-time college dropout seeking salvation from a future in food service, you could become a new person, another creature. That through such an osmotic process, a deeper understanding of other lives and lifeways could be forged.

In Preskitt, while you waited to be illuminated, you began to find that daily existence unfolded at a slower pace than it did back in Portland, at speeds that mirrored natural rhythms: long stretches of sameness, punctuated suddenly by motion. The beauty of brown desert hills, wood that gives off scent after the sun sets, the sound of long train horns in dusty air. The first time you rode your bike at night, a clunky steel-frame, slowly up a long hill toward home, the stars were like giant glimmering eggs in a vast black pool: beacons of light and of life beyond the limits of your own. They had never seemed hung so close to the earth, or so important. As you rode each day to school through flocks of crows, through the whispery cicada-pulse of summer neighborhood streets lazy with heat, there was spaciousness: room between houses and businesses, room between roads. There was room down each little alleyway for lost cars, lost tourists, slender young cottonwoods and dumpsters alike. The sun had space to find each shy sliver of shade and set it uncurling. And then surprises: after lying all day in the sun outside your door, a prone and seemingly dead lizard would shoot its tongue across a rock to stab a stinkbug.

This all created a focus you found comforting: the fact that you could see for miles across the land from any high point, the apparent need for really only a few select things: some shade, some water, some food. The perspective had a way of clearing out whatever else existed between you, a creature in this place, and the huge clear sky above it: providence, the gods, existential stillness, whatever you'd like to call it. You could sit in the open air exposed and feel the sun work its strength into your skin, carving wrinkles, soaking your melanin, pulling you to the surface of yourself. It burnt you clean of any shadow corners, pockets, false selves you brought with you when you arrived. Maybe Molly Melanoma and not Polly Polyp would kill you, which would be fine. At night, the sun dissipated totally, leaving a clear surface for the stars, meteor showers, and comets to light their maps instead. Living in the desert, you began to feel that if you could erase yourself enough, your various moods and agendas, needs and desires, you could simply become a pair of ears to hear, eyes to see, and hands to translate: purer, uncluttered, uncompromised. But see, hear, and translate what, and to whom? You opened your eyes wider, put your ear to the dirt.

Preskitt, you learned, makes a fairly successful "recovery town," recent substance abusers flying or busing into this arid zone from all fifty states to kick drugs or dry out from city life, either in residential group homes or Preskitt-based NOLS (National Outdoor

Leadership School) courses taking them farther out into nature. Perhaps because of its quietness relative to other American cities, or its relative bucolic isolation—orange rolling rocks and flat wide blue above—the success rate for people rediscovering normal rhythms of living, and making good change, is high. You can't explain why a cactus would calm, or why the site of a javelina snorting brutishly through the brush could soothe, but it does. Light erupts early and bright across a horizon, bathing the hills, aching cold and frosty, in sudden heat. It's hard to stay inside.

So you stepped out early every day from your newly rented above-garage studio, rode past the Neoclasssical Revival-style courthouse, the brightly painted Victorian homes behind it, past the otherworldly craggy granite rising in mounds, and gazed out toward the round-topped green mountains behind that en route to school. Once at school, you sat down in your classes to learn about the land, about the border, about stories and the psychological borders between people. Your mind, like this new land, opened out widened, and for the first time you couldn't find the ends of it.

You took a catering job, because a body must still afford to eat while the mind grows. The kitchen was hot, and you cut your hair down to an inch so you could breathe while you chopped vegetables, measured flours, oiled meats for the oven, and mixed huge vats of salads and lemonades for the well-dressed older guests at local events. One day your kitchen put on black and white uniforms and carried all the food in silver tubs and trays to the van, there to wind down into the center of town to the nearby pioneer museum. The reason Arizona was named Arizona, you learned while you wandered through the main exhibit en route to a bathroom, was the jamming together of "arid" and *zona*, the arid zone, a place of no water. You learned that alongside childbirth, the most frequent way pioneer women in the Old West died was from catching their skirts on fire at their cookstoves, too modest to tie them up to safety. The tour didn't say how non-pioneer women died most frequently, but you suspected it had something to do with the pioneers.

The term "erasure" has been used, in the American West and around the world, to describe the effects of colonization on indigenous peoples—you didn't need the college classes to know this by now. The names on the I-17 and 69 road signs hint at local histories: Bloody Basin Road. Skull Valley. Wrangler's Roost. But then there's Black Canyon City. Bumble Bee. Carefree. Strawberry. Lake Pleasant. Old antagonism jammed close, now, against clusters of retirement communities and quaintness. If you pay any kind of attention, you can feel this twinning, the pleasure of sensory beauty hard up against and burrowed into horror. For some people, especially the more recently arrived and air-conditioned, the arid zone may seem to be a kind of paradise, a wombing oven of recovery and respite; for others, the oven has incinerated, though not particularly through fault of the oven. As you became acquainted more closely with the spaces the first peoples inhabited and, in smaller number, still inhabit here, you realized you would never, at least in this iteration of life, experience this land as they have: knowing intimately, interdependently, for the whole length of life, and through centuries of shared knowledge beforehand, how to coax food from hard soil, or the subtle smell of incoming rain.

In the middle of the Grand Canyon, while your small class rustled away at dinner-making tasks at a downriver campsite, you sat alone on the plastic open-air toilet at the far end of Horseshoe Mesa, rising, seemingly suspended, from the center of emptiness. Your new home, you were starting to know, was ancient, despite its recent status in the New World. If you let yourself, you could feel its residues. As your shit dropped from the warmth of your living body into nowhere, with no splash or resonant smack, your mind dropped into silence. Time slowed. The canyon is still sparsely peopled within severely motionless orange-, brown-, and yellow-layered walls. On a faraway path, maybe you'll be lucky to see a tiny donkey humping forward like an ant toward the flat blue sky, or a condor circling high above with an eye toward fresh-dead dining. Feelings of absorption stretch and linger. Contemporary tourists pay dearly for this oblivion-romance, with pricey flights and tours, or with their bodies after days of tromping: pulled muscles, broken bones, blood blisters. Some even go beyond ego-annihilation to find complete physical obliteration, via selfie-stick cliff toppling, mountain lion lunchtime, good old-fashioned dehydration, and more. The notorious local history tome *Over the Edge: Death in the Canyon* is dedicated to describing each of the five hundred recorded fatal misadventures in the canyon from the 1890s to the present, which helps you realize the power of this place to crush or reward you.

"You have to respect it," says your friend Lucky Louie, who himself was nearly eaten once by mountain lions, yet who still descends the canyon several times weekly to lead tours, campouts, and rim-to-rim endurance hikes for tourists he variably enjoys or respects far less than the place he takes them. He's right: once you drop below the rim—and only 1 percent of all Grand Canyon visitors do—you find a world so very much *itself* that the only sound around you anywhere is the breeze clattering through woody yucca stalks or its whispery breath through desert grass. You can find yourself forgetting your history, your memory, the languages you thought were the ones connecting you to the world.

Farther down at the bottom of the canyon, deeper below your sight, is Supai, the thousand-plus-years-old home to the Havasu Baaja, or Havasupai, an indigenous tribe of roughly 640. Some still live there, in the village at the base of a brilliant blue-green waterfall. Hippie kids, including your friend Louie, will make the rough eight-mile hike down to swim, but you don't imagine you will; the settlement remains under threat from too many forces for you to feel good about visiting. You imagine what they might feel if they saw you bathing, sunburnt, in their waterfall: yet another reminder of tourists and their trash, their abandoned dogs, which must be dealt with or adopted, and the Grand Canyon Uranium Mine itching to reopen after a twenty-year moratorium meant to stabilize an ecological area so close to the crucial

Colorado River. Environmentalists and capitalists both lobby their legislators, as do the paper-chasers who own the mine and ache for a profit as unstable and ravenous as the element itself. Are you, by accident and ignorance, complicit? Who do you vote for, and what do you buy, bankrolled by whom?

Would that, one day, you think, there would be no "I," "you," or "they."

A little ribbon of road, real trouble for distractible drivers, leads you out of this canyon to offer yet another perspective: a gaze out into the vast Verde Valley, which gives you the impression you are part of infinity. These lands mirror the oceans once contained in them, reminding you how even seeming stability (like rock) and flux (sea salt water) interchange over time, which reminds you (yet again) just how connected all earthscapes and the creatures within them are.

At the top of this road, a lesson in timescape: you funnel suddenly into an old mining town filled with tall wooden homes, built close between blocky stone staircases. These stairs zigzag up through side yards to connect each road farther up and down the hill between the homes, like stitching you might pull tight to collapse the town in on itself. In its heyday, the buildings of Jerome housed copper mining offices, brothels, prisons, bars, and a giant, still intact old asylum. The asylum, with its structural "good bones" and depressing plethora of rooms, now houses the town's fanciest tourist hotel; the brothel, a gift shop. The bars, different in name and plumbing, still serve the same whiskey to make time slow or speed up as desired.

At the far end of Jerome's hairpin turns, past the motorcycle strip and some lonely patches of prickly pear, there is a parking lot for the now defunct Gold King Copper Mine. You can walk from there out past the chain-link Do Not Enter sign. On the mine tailings' narrow footpath, now littered with smelting leftovers—beautiful and debatably toxic, melted and twisted bronzed ribs—you can follow bobcat prints to the end of the hillside that looks over what feels like all of northern Arizona.

Clouds cruise slowly, flat-bottomed as if sliding on a single pane of glass. Sometimes the clouds don't move at all, and it's as if you are staring at a painting, as if time has frozen. More than rarely, you can see a hawk drawing shadows on the land below, striping dark onto light, making patterns, slowing, and then repeating. You can't actually find the spot where the mine machinery plunged down into the earth, over and over again, forfeiting many attendant humans, in quest of "value." You scan the valley for it. It's got to be there, or up here in this hill.

But look: down there is Tuzigoot, theorized to be an abandoned ancient Sinagua settlement perched on the highest point in the valley, its small stone rooms swathed around a central, laddered stack of a lookout tower. The tourist placards ringing the perimeter of the structures along the new paved path claim that it's a mystery why those peoples left: perhaps invasion, perhaps the need to trade. Or perhaps the Verde Valley, at that time apparently more "verdant," finally dried out and corn became harder to grow; the visitor center can't even keep their own straggling sample corn stalks and squash vines alive in the educational demo plot.

When you stepped into the centralmost room at Tuzigoot for the first time, tucked under another room though not underground, you took its shadows, somehow, into your mind. You tried to cover up a sudden leaky eye with your shirtsleeve, leaned on the ladder.

"PMS, I guess," you told your school group, palms up as if waiting for information: mysterious cycles, you insinuate; some things never change. One teacher you had wrote a poem about her PMS: the sorrow coming on from her body's acknowledgement, as she aged, that the future of her was monthly evaporating in each bloodied toilet paper scrap: each woman only gets so many eggs to seed new generations into the world to come. You aren't thinking about this as you push outside again into the sun, not fast enough. You think about generativity and the loss of a potential future, years later, when you take your brother with you to visit the ruins again. You leave him to wander so you can find the bathroom. He meets you at the end of the loop trail, maybe twelve minutes later, and asks if the under-the-ladder room was the room you'd felt so bad in before, because your brother, a big-tech employee in New York now, not prone to the woo-woo, says he feels terrible in that room, too.

"Was there a massacre in there?" he asks.

You hate to say that "likely" is on the tip of your tongue in reply, so you tell him you don't know.

Not too long after you hiked out of the Grand Canyon and then out of Tuzigoot, you took a job dishwashing at a local not-quite-cowboy, more artsy bar. The bar, beautifully appointed with deep-hued hardwoods and tapestry-sized paintings of the land and of ravens, served people with some money, and sometimes they drank too much and got a little entitled: they wanted the cute girl in the blue rubber gloves (you) to come talk to them from the back. One man demanded that you sing him "Happy Birthday," a request you refused—easy enough to go back to the steamy dishpit and feign busyness, deafness in the noise of kitchen clatter. But at the end of one shift, the dishes ran out and you sat down for your free shift-drink to wait for the cooks to finish putting away leftovers, for the bartenders to close their tills so you could mop your way out. Also sitting late at the bar was a big spender, a bad tipper, bitching to the barback about hippie environmentalists. They impede business, he said, and he ran one.

"Am I right?" he asked you, perhaps thinking you were preprogrammed to agree with all customers.

You shrugged. It doesn't matter much to you if the world goes to dust, you said: a desolate desert is where you want to end up in any case, living or dead. In fact all of us will end up dead no matter what, but you thought that he might care. You pointed at his wedding ring. Perhaps he had kids. Legacy.

But he shook his head. If the earth was all used up this next century, he and his would simply "hop a ship to Mars."

Erasure—91

That was why he made money, he said, and why it was important. "So you have control over your destiny. So you can survive."

He picked up one of the dollars he'd tipped on a beer, pointed to the eye on the pyramid, sun brimming forth behind it.

Light, the metaphoric symbol of the divine, you told him, confounds science in its apparently dual nature as both particle and wave.

"You're a hippie!" he exclaimed.

By a similar stroke, you said, living creatures are mysteriously both entities of themselves and at once interdependent on the other many entities to which they are attached. Independence, the way he is speaking, is an unreality.

Besides, you said, why create a massively complicated system for survival in space when it's simple to live here, where it's set up for us? You motioned toward the mountains beyond the tall restaurant windows, standing quiet in the dark. "Not to mention beautiful."

But you can't stop progress, he said. It's human nature to explore, expand. "Go forth and populate the earth," he quoted, biblically.

At the end of times, at least as you remembered it, sitting on your bar stool and reaching back to childhood catechism, the Abrahamic god of population growth would snap the universal threads that held the spherical construction of the world together, hell would drop like a dead weight into the middle of the earth's molten core and heaven could then float upward, unmoored by the habits of the weak. Maybe that's why, you thought, so many of this religious bent aren't environmentalists—it's all just a waiting game anyway, a future you can't fight, and heaven-above-earth seems the epitome of loveliness, not like cold black space.

You shuddered to think of a home on a spaceship, another closed-up Noah's Ark: only pitchy, inky window-fodder visible, scattered with lights so distant they would seem like deep-sea death debris. Then sterile metal interiors, zero-gravity bone density, and tasteless algae meals. Once, you dreamt of drifting in an astronaut suit away from the spaceship that was your home, breathing tube detached and trailing like a tapeworm behind you. As you floated further from your source of warmth, community, purpose, into deep darkness, the sense of loss and cold was crushing. You craved other life to stave off the nothingness, to keep the borders of yourself intact: your loves, your links, your repulsions, your relation to all other matter which seemed now just a far extended and quickly departing part of the same you.

In some native Southwest creation stories, people, or at least their people, emerged from a hole in the earth to reside in this world. A hole that must also have been deep, dark, and cold. What a shock it must have been, then, to meet the Southwest sun, the bright light that browns the skin golden before bleaching bones. Perhaps such a contrast would inspire a hesitation to overwhelm, to swarm carelessly like ants, like rabbits, or a virus—or like so many empire-inclined peoples.

Your bartender friend turned from his polishing to look at you, eyebrows raised, as if pleading for the biblical bar patron *not* to populate the world any further, to cease speaking of spaceships. And perhaps the patron could feel the bartender's coldness or yours, or deepening night. Eventually he put on his coat and gloves and left, and you went back into the kitchen to mop.

You'd become friendly with a young painter named Desmond, although you're not sure he considered you a friend: you are white. You tried to see yourself through his eyes, and the picture wasn't lovely. He himself was half white but also half Hopi, and he was keenly aware of what ancestors who looked like yours did to his. Also what lawmakers and cowboys and businessmen who look like you now continue to do to people who look like him. Nevertheless you hung out sometimes: took walks, talked about his art, drank beer.

When you had sex, Desmond turned your face to the veneer-paneled wall of your studio with his cheek, so you were both looking off in the same direction rather than at each other. You wondered if he hated you while he was inside of you. You knew it was possible to hate what you were inside of. In a studio in the back of his family's property, Desmond showed you how he had angled a film projector at a wall and traced the figures of deer, trees, and tribal elders from early black-and-white photos onto large canvasses. Then, with paint, he spliced the deer and trees with power lines, armed the elders with machine guns in place of bows and arrows, and placed them behind shadowed foliage, hiding at the ready before three incoming brown wooden ships, crosses on their white sails blazing red.

In his 1910 "Proposing the Moral Equivalent of War," philosopher William James theorized that "people" (which ones, he did not specify) seem to find life without the intense, immediate, existential grappling of war, well, boring. And he was not the only one: Francisco Cantú, Cristina Rivera Garza, and Alessandro Baricco (among others, I'm sure) have all lately contemplated whether the risk and excitement of war might eventually be replaced with some other kind of productive human endeavor.

The question is, do we want to?

Lt. Col. Dave Grossman, former army ranger and West Point psychology professor, draws uneasy parallels between the thrill of sex and military-sanctioned aggression. Carrying a gun, for a soldier, Grossman claims, is like an erection, and shooting it is akin to orgasmic discharge. Across the pond back in Europe, the French have been known to call orgasm *la petite mort*, "the little death," referring to the obliteration of the self or consciousness at climax.

▧ Which seems to be the delicate line, a question of quantity: how much erasure is generative, leading to life, versus the type that tips too far into totality? Though erasure, death itself, is a neutral condition, naturally concluding every earthly being, the *how* and *how much* of death matters.

The gun, Kit Carson's gun and Custer's gun, all the guns of the Spanish and English and French, wait to erase, like arrows which perhaps must work more patiently, or atom and hydrogen bombs which wait most precariously. All the weapons wait, and beyond them unfurls the future. You wait to see what all these weapons will do. Like the master story writer Anton Chekhov warned, a storyteller doesn't write a gun into a narrative unless he means to fire it by the end. But there are so many guns, and so many have been so long locked-and-loaded: if they are all fired, there will be no story anymore.

Down the street from your house in Presskitt is a neighborhood thick with cicada churn. Titus, a former Marine, lives there, in a mostly empty house. Titus is in his thirties, but whether on the early or late end of that time spectrum is a mystery to you. His beard is that of a man in his forties, his face well weathered from the sun, and he told you once that when he dies, he will already be the color of the dirt to which he returns. His muscular body ripples, with calves like cable wire motoring dirt-crusted feet, now flat from walking everywhere thin-sandaled or bare. You've never seen him in a car. One year he walked to Mexico with just a donkey, then back.

A former Marine, in fact a former Special Ops Marine, Titus could mesmerize you with the intensity of his gaze and snap your neck meanwhile, but he wouldn't do that now. A few years back, he reformed into a peacenik. Clarity is important: Titus is not a peacenik because he shies from addressing conflict, but by deliberate philosophical choice to address it differently. In his backyard garden, he grows crops to eat and to share with groups that feed the homeless. When he bought a larger plot of land out of town, he began to supply a cafe downtown with organics. In Titus's garden, there is water, light, and a mix of heterogeneous nutrients: the simplest ingredients for growth. He's not doing anything differently from centuries of people before him: he's just gardening.

And in his old-school version of gardening, it pays to study. Mint, rosemary, and lemongrass repel mosquitos, but only marigolds also discourage rabbits. Basil will deter mosquitoes and houseflies, while lavender rebuffs moths and fleas. Oregano gives ground cover—shade and humidity—for peppers. Your job as a gardener, he explains, is not to fry the whole garden with Roundup, risking total eventual ruination, but to coax and repel, balance and include, equalize.

He shows your school group his composting toilet.

"Uh-oh," he says, holding up a particularly well-preserved turd, "someone ate Cheetos." His shit, which does not contain artificial ingredient remnants and is mostly made of plants, heats up and rots quickly with the rest of the veggie matter discarded from his garden. After a few months he can turn it, spread it back over hungry living matter. Rinse, repeat. There's no impulse to impede or endlessly postpone fatality, but rather to follow it and help it be fruitful. Draw respectfully close to it and learn.

Your friend Louie, like your husband Tim, rides motorcycles. Unlike Tim, who you have worried about in late-night imaginings of roadside carnage, Louie actually has crashed. Riding home from the canyon one night with his friend on the back, he took a turn in the dark too fast and went off into bramble, throwing both boys from the bike. Eric, somehow landing safely, called the EMTs, who eventually flight-lifted Louie to Flagstaff for surgery to put his guts back inside him, gave him a transfusion, set his bones.

Louie was also almost eaten once. Long before he had the bike-wreck, blood still swirling in his eyes, he told you about it. He and the same friend, Eric, were hiking in part of the Colorado Plateau where desert and woods begin to meet. They'd gotten lost, off their trail onto another somehow, and then onto another, until the way back home was anybody's guess. As dusk was falling, a mountain lion stepped into the clearing where they had chosen to set up impromptu camp. They froze. The lion began to circle. Louie knew they couldn't outrun it. He was just about to make noise and shake his arms, make himself appear bigger like you are supposed to, when another lion appeared. Then another. Lions often hunt alone, but for whatever reason, not tonight. Eric, on the verge of shitting himself, began to sing. A goodbye-cruel-world song: if you gotta go, after all, make the noise you want to on the way. But the lions didn't approach any further: they stood and stared, tails slowly flicking. Looking around, Louie began to sing too. The big cats sat slowly down into front-paw cross-legs. All night long the lost boys sang, and eventually the lions lay down around them in a loose circle. The boys were afraid to stop, so they just kept on singing whatever came to mind, one starting when the other stopped. At dawn the lions got up one by one and left. The exhausted boys wept and hugged and stumbled their way back, contemporary Daniels stepped from the Lion's Den. Louie became an environmental advocate. Now he lives on a cheap piece of land near the canyon in a Tuffshed, drinking rainwater, catching sun, voting down uranium mine initiatives, telling the tourists he guides every day about balance. Often there must be death. Sometimes there is mercy. There is power in mercy, and in curiosity, you think, after hearing Louie's story, to transform from the primal motivation to live at all cost to something else: compassion, a consideration of the price of survival. Or whether there is another survival than just the survival of one body. Or one family of bodies. Or one society of bodies. Or one species. A planetful.

At what point does the cost of physical survival cease to outweigh another thing—a celestial survival—a unity many religious and spiritualists claim to trust, that the singular soul reaches beyond this momentary set of skin, this liminal lump of tenuously joined-up bones?

Once, your dad asked if you feared death. You said no, only you feared not finishing all the wonderful things you wanted to do beforehand. Then you asked him.

He replied that he'd just say thanks for the opportunity to have been here, to have seen and lived all this.

This is what you think when you think about your own bones, come to rest in a tree: the line where life stops and becomes something else, the divine. You'd like whatever remains of you in this life to lie in a tidal wave of other elements: scorching sun, beating wind, and birds. The membranes can separate, dissolve, amass, reabsorb into the blanket of other elements from which we all derive. Let the birds take you piecemeal back to scatter into the land you love: a finger for Flagstaff and a toe for Tucson, your pharynx for Phoenix and your pulmonary artery straight back to Preskitt. Then, you think, dump the rest around Ajo, the scorched and lime-whitened hills before these "united" states run off the map into Mexico. Start again there.

This is what you mean to say when you say "erasure" is not a kind of suicide-romance of yours, which some readers may, by now, be thinking. Rather, you fathom this erasure as a kind of communion: a closed book ready to reopen. A bellows exhausted, waiting to refill with air, when you begin the long drive out of Tuzigoot, or awaken with your Grand Canyon class and begin the long walk up. Into what? Into future.

◂

You don't live in desert all the time anymore, but you think of it often and, on many grim days, long for it. From behind your desk, instead of a city or a neighborhood, you see wide dirt, pocked with bramble, distant mountains, and a sky as blue as the sea, freeways spacious enough for the shiny giant trucks you never saw in Portland's parade of 1970s Volvos and Volkswagens, paint-chipped and rusty, then Tim and his mother on motorcycles and you following in the chase car: up and down the hills you all go, their bodies before you, almost floating on their bikes, sunset catching in the filaments of their hair, weightless at the peak of each hill.

As the seasons change around your desk now, your new window in some old city, you know what Arizona is doing: the air turns from roasting dry heat to a gathering of moist clouds, swelling.

You can close your eyes and remember: a tarantula had made its slow-stepping way across your front yard that first day of monsoons, on migration, your friends said, south. You were gathering your things, bag over shoulder, to go to the bank, when you heard thunder. You stuck your hand skyward from the porch and felt a drop.

I'll just wait until this is over, you thought, leaning the bike back down on the railing, settling cross-legged on the porch swing.

Within moments, crackling thunder had unzipped the sky and a deluge fell down in a sheet, fast and hard, drops huge and wet, the whole mess so thick you couldn't see through it and so heavy you could smell the heat brought up from the dirt as the silver wetness pummeled down. A river formed in the street, and a child's plastic trike raced down it amidst mud and stick debris.

You never did make it to the bank, as the first rain, always the longest, went on like this for over an hour.

Later you would find all the empty dirt-canals in town clogged with loud, brown water, fast enough to carry branches, baby carriages, boats, and apparently bodies, away to the aqueducts, and from there, who knows: to the next place.

Below the clouds
The people think quietly of (still) quiet things:
The dark parts of themselves,
The hollows of the land
Where an eel would have waited,
Now a cougar,
A mountain lion, sleek with sweat and hardened.

Let it rise from you and start again
Shaped like something else entirely.

Drive (III)

En route to the "New Rez," we passed by the turnoff for Canyon de Chelly. Here the Diné, known by whites as Navajo people, resisted capture by Kit Carson's army in the late 1800s, retreating into rock wall mazes and evading capture for months. But Carson would not be released from service until he'd carried out his general's order to "relocate" the local natives. So he stopped negotiating and ordered his men to burn their crops, chop down their beloved peachtree groves. Midwinter, full of sorrow and rage, the starving Diné emerged from the canyon and surrendered, commencing a closely patrolled Long Walk for hundreds of miles across the desert to Bosque Redondo. There, at a kind of prison reservation with few resources and a shattered way of life, it was four years of disease and despair before they could walk back.

In my school textbooks growing up, the Long Walk was rolled into one paragraph along with the Trail of Tears. When I moved to Arizona, I began to learn more. As a fourth-time college undergraduate, I drove with an anthropologist to Nahata Dziil, a new reservation parcel chaptered in 1991. Smaller than the Navajo "Big Rez," the largest indigenous reservation left in the United States, it still felt vast as we passed cliffs, rocks, and wiry churro sheep. The anthropologist I accompanied had worked in this community for decades, documenting oral history. She'd gotten a grant to help the schoolkids here preserve community stories on video in the face of native language loss and aging elders. That the people here have struggled so much has so much to do with her ancestors and mine, European genes threading silently through us. I'm scared and ashamed to see what our people have done to these people, and yet, after years of running from things that confuse me, I feel driven to witness.

Spaced apart across a seeming sea of land are hogans, traditional Diné homes, mud or stone and roundish in the reliable way of time's tendency to repeat. The new government-built houses in New Rez, by contrast, are tucked closely together as in any other American suburb: rectangular with angled roofs, flammably wooden. Some have a porch, like the one I stayed at with the anthropologist, where crickets creaked hot and hungry in the long yellow grasses at sunset. In the evening, on the porch, we tried chatting, though I found the anthropologist gruff. Even in her spare time, she was pragmatic. She didn't wander about wondering about the world: she trained her dogs on search-and-rescue missions to save lost hikers from recreation gone awry in various regional canyons.

When we woke and joined the classroom, I watched the students work, leaning over computers. They'd already recorded their elders' stories. They'd filmed the B-roll footage they wanted to pair with those interviews. Now they listened through headphones as they snipped and spliced, rolling the films of their grandparents' faces backward and forward using trackpads. Predictably, none of them needed my help with the "arc" or "plot" or "tension," those narrative devices Euro-American writers so often use to separate (artificially?) one story from another (and which I, an English major by then, was trained to think about). Instead they just needed help with the tech, and because my computer skills were paltry, my job became simply to fetch the anthropologist. When I stepped outside on my breaks, I wondered how many new kinds of language the kids were going to have to learn in order to be heard. Was our project a useful resuscitation of endangered conversation—or yet more mandated conversion?

Afterward we went to a picnic. The anthropologist chatted with community members she'd known for years, but I found I didn't know what to say. My questions and small talk even struck me as annoying. So after a while I just stood and watched the kids race, arms pumping, uphill and downhill, joyously free of the classroom.

"Are you planning to teach?" the anthropologist asked me on the ride home, broaching my debatable English-degree career options. The way she asked was skeptical, as I was too after my fumbling performance with the eighth graders.

"Well . . ." I said. "Before I teach, I should probably become a better student."

Behind the western hills, the evening sun slid down to the place where sunrise awaited.

Magnet Man

I shift from foot to foot. Both my feet hurt. I'm packing magnets at my dad's factory, back up North, and the rubber mats meant to cushion my joints from the floor don't help.

A little to my left is bald-topped Tom, a little to my right is chatty Candy, and in front of me is a concrete wall. If I go further to the left of Tom, the warehouse door opens out onto the parking lot, where my dad eats lunch in his car. I understand why he does. He's a salesman—albeit one trained in the physics of ferrite, who draws complex equations for his clients in China—so he spends a lot of time on the phone: yak, yak, yak. I'd hate it: I'd rather pack, although I'm not allowed to pack the rare-earth bundles, so strong they could crush my fingertips without enough cardboard between to keep their relentless attractions apart. Plus, the packing jobs I do are not always so good anyway: a few broken shipments have come back in the mail, and sometimes I wonder if I ever properly learned to count. Candy shows me how to weigh the smaller pellet-magnets into batches, and that helps a little.

For as long as I can remember, my dad has worked in this field. When I was little, he used to run factories: machines pouring water over metal blades to cool while they cut, converting raw matter into magnet. Now he sells the attractive and repulsive pieces of metal for a boss he dislikes. I live, for the moment, at his house in his spare room, and he gives me sixty dollars a week to clean it, out of kindness, as I am broke. I pack at his factory while I think about my ex-fiancé. What a dumb word, I think, fiancé: a label for the in-between. It had felt fake when I said it to people, and I'd felt like a liar when I went to try on dresses: something wasn't quite right in the idea of marrying Jonathan at the time I'd agreed to. But I still miss him. Beyond the plain gray factory walls and the parking lot and my dad in the car are several open tall-grass fields, like there always are at Dad's factories, and I wish I could wander there alone with my thoughts instead of slapping on packing labels, then slapping on my best attempt at a smile when Candy comes to chat. But I can't. I have to make money.

When I walked back into the Portland International Airport after my impending marriage collapsed, the famously green-bubble carpet looked suspiciously, for the first time, like barf. When I got to baggage claim, my whole little family was there. Mum had remarried into a tiny new apartment where there was no room for visitors, and my brother explained his disinclination to host me this way:

"Every time you visit, you drop your bags on the floor, and they explode your stuff all over my house." He made the motion of a little big bang with his hands, fingers blooming slowly outward. "Plus, I don't know when you'd leave."

Certainly, jobs can be tough to find in Portland, what with the influx of people just like me (youngish, educated, artsy) competing en masse in similar industries. But I felt like leaving everywhere all the time now, I almost said to my brother—and after Preskitt and then L.A. and then the breakup, even my running off to Peru, a place I'd always dreamt of visiting, didn't proffer any joy now—so not to worry; I doubted I'd stick around long. But that might have sounded too grim to a sibling.

I hadn't seen my dad since I told him, over the phone in an argument three months before, that he was a "conditionally loving parent," and yet he was the one who offered me a guest room to land in: a room with a tiny twin bed, tucked into a suburb safe from homelessness, half an hour north of Portland.

When I first moved into Dad's, I'd found a job for two weeks at a sushi bar. Irritatingly, in addition to the tedious commute to it, the sushi bar made me split my shift: work three hours during lunch and three during dinner, with two hours unpaid between. During that little slice of time, I would eat my own cheap non-sushi lunch and wander the city. In the spring rain I could revisit all my old stomping grounds: coffee shops, clothing shops, libraries. But after my travels, the light-rail moved too slowly between stops. The beggars' stories all seemed like ruses. My dimes wouldn't stack up to stabilize their lives against the gray-blanket sky any more than the sushi job would stack up to help me find new love and a meaningful life direction again. But I was in a city, nonetheless, full of potential. Which was what Los Angeles had, once, seemed full of, too.

Once upon a time I lived in Arizona, and so did Jonathan. Jonathan who tagged along with my friends and charmed me with his dimples. Jonathan with huge eyes that seemed to comprehend everything, and a smile like he was really happy. He was quitting school. He was about to abandon his college experiment (cacti, javelina) to return to SoCal (beaches, bike rides). He was silly. He was compassionate. When he left for L.A., I missed him, and wandered around the Walmart in my little Arizona cowboy town alone at 3 a.m. I was graduating. I was aimless. I was tired of my dishwashing job and my perpetually damp, swollen hands. On my trips to visit Jonathan, the City of Angels bloomed in ten-drilled trumpet vines, was framed by bougainvillea. Jonathan's family lived in a cluttered and hilly part of town; the crumbly streets were hell on my suspension, but because they wound together to meet the mythic old Sunset Strip, it all felt worthwhile to explore. Between the grime and the traffic, mission-style and modern theaters, hidden swatches of land had been tucked away into fatefully named parks: Echo, Elysian. The Hollywood history plastered onto posters and mega-murals suffused the imagination, inspired an eager energy: fantasies could come true there. And the sea, just an hour away, concealed altogether unfamiliar further universes below the darkened, tight-stretched mirror of its surface. Like a siren song, the mystery of it pulled and eventually extracted me from the desert. Arizona had a dishwashing job. L.A. had . . . who knew what?

Jonathan wanted me to marry him.

I moved as if in a tractor beam.

"Here's a scarf from Peru," I said when I moved into Dad's.

"When did you go to Peru?" he asked.

"After L.A.," I said.

Given that I hadn't been speaking to him then, I hadn't told him of my travels, and apparently no one else had, either. I half expected an eruption now, as from the white-capped volcano overlooking Arequipa. But I had, after all, brought him a gift.

"Oh. Well . . ." He fingered the fuzzy llama fur quietly. I imagined he was deciding whether or not to pick a fight.

"It's a nice scarf," he concluded, wrapping the soft red strip around his neck.

Peru: Land of *National Geographic* color photos. Land of mountains rising from tufted clouds. Land of Incas, conquistadores, knotted-rope quipus, pan flutes, canyons, pit mines, and ancient ruins we can't now replicate. Blocks are stacked together into buildings in Cuzco without mortar, so tight you can't slip even a knife blade between. Some conspiracy theorists think the ruins were built by ancient aliens: future space-born extraterrestrial versions of ourselves come back in time to aid us through history.

In Peru now, I want to tell my dad but don't, some people live in metal cubes. Outside the unleaded-gas scooter stench of Lima, through the windows of our air-conditioned bus, makeshift structures began to dot the land as my travel partner and I rode: notorious, tiny and tin, just big enough for one person to curl up to sleep in. But these shacks, draped in laundry, seemed to be used as family homes.

Diane, who'd joined me from Santa Fe, came with me to stay on Taquile, a giant island in the midst of Lake Titicaca, where the residents had no heat in their sections of the homes—but our guest rooms did—and the locals carried loads bigger than our bodies on their backs. On Uros, the islands of floating reeds there, the indigenous inhabitants were small, living on the littlest salt-dried fish. They traded these fish, too, for rice. They made crafts for tourists like us and sang-clapped us folk songs to thank our group for coming until they ran out of breath in the bright sun, in the thin air.

On the train to Machu Picchu's base town, children chased each moving car. "¡Da-me!" they called, with hands gesturing to mouths, and we threw our white boxes of prepackaged train food out the windows to them, along with all the other well-fed Euro-American tourists who were also catapulting theirs.

Before I ran out of money, in Arequipa, Diane and I shared a gourmet lime-cooked rare beef meal, discussed our observations—about minicabs, copper mines, condors, and colonialism—then swapped lost-love stories when the our pisco sours took hold. A protest group began to march by, just beyond the restaurant gate, chaperoned by riot-gear-clad soldiers and their assault rifles. Diane and I agreed, against the eery silence of this protest: we'd both seen new things on this trip, but the most important thing we were learning was that we were lucky.

After I pack magnets each day, if my feet don't ache too badly, I jog around Dad's neighborhood, reaching for and stockpiling endorphins against the oncoming autumn. Sometimes my friends from Portland drive out to pick me up for drinks, which is nice because after I swapped sushi serving for magnet packing, I don't get into the city too often. When it's raining too much to run, or my friends have deemed my dad's house too far to drive, I clean the house or read. If the house is clean already and I'm too sad to read, I give up and let the memories come: how it all tumbled together and then apart before I could understand it. Out past the window of my room at Dad's, past peals of early thunder, I peel my memories back past Peru.

After Arizona.

To the salty warm city by the sea.

I could almost feel the dip in Jonathan's chest under my fingertips. My love was forgetful. In L.A. he ran late by hours. We'd moved into the studio in his parents' backyard to save on rent, but it meant I had to go into their main house each time I had to pee. When Jonathan went to work at a summer camp three hours north, I carpooled each day with his dad to their law firm to transcribe depositions and watch lawyers dive under desks to finish their phone calls when the San Andreas fault shimmied. I gossiped with coworkers who'd all known Jonathan for years. Then I carpooled back home with his dad, ate dinner with his mom. I spent all my spare time with Jonathan's people, but not with him. In his absence, it seemed as if some part of myself was somehow sucked away too. I didn't read: I watched movies. I didn't make friends: I had his. On days I slipped out to drive aimlessly, to a beach or a bookshop alone, I felt less alone than at other times, but I saw this loneliness more clearly. Part of the problem with desire is the subtlety with which it works: the cognitive dissonance you feel as you're pulled toward a thing, as you slip into its trajectory, almost without noticing. At some point, if you don't want to be in orbit anymore, you must recall that you're a person, in possession of free will, and do something.

One morning in L.A., I woke after a dream. I'd been swimming in the sea, pulled by kindly dolphins' dorsal fins along a diamond-sparkling surf. The water below was so blue it hurt my eyes: Arizona turquoise, quiet desert skies. I was relieved, fulfilled, and yet Jonathan was nowhere in sight. When I realized, waking slowly, where I was waking, my joy drained palpably from my body.

I understood: I hated my life, or at least this version of it.

I thanked the dolphins mentally, told Jonathan sorry, and took the I-10 to Arizona. When Arizona was emptier than I remembered, I called in my frequent-flyer miles, called Diane, and hopped a plane. To break free. Change course. Do something different, I hoped.

In the Peruvian highlands I met Catherine, the only stranger I've ever invited to my table. When she walked in the door of the only pizza shop in Cuzco, I knew she was American: her tall stature, her boot-cut jeans, the San Francisco-style slouch cap all gave her away before she spoke, asking in neutral English how the food was. Since Diane was at a ruins site and I was dining alone, Catherine's openness and confidence intrigued me.

She was an Apache helicopter pilot, she said, on mandatory leave for a month. "You have to work hard," she said, "then take a break, then come back." Otherwise you burn out. Make mistakes.

People have a rhythm, just like everything else.

Catherine said she'd learned to fly before she got her driver's license. She ran missions in the Middle East now. In her spare time she explored the planet, and she was applying with NASA to fly above it.

Beside her story, my exploration felt unimportant, but when she asked, I still told her—a complete stranger—of my love-life fail. And that somewhere between Puno and Cuzco, Jonathan had stopped replying to my friendly "checking in" e-mails, which I just couldn't stop myself from sending, even after I left L.A.

Then Catherine told me another story, about a colleague in the military she'd hated. She'd decided not to get him in trouble when she had the chance, to have compassion, and all the better: He showed up as her commander in another unit. And treated her well.

Every action has repercussions that vibrate forward, returning like a boomerang, she said. Neither good nor bad. Simply true.

"Remember that," she said. "Nothing ever ends. Things only shift shapes and become new starts."

Recursion. Eternal return. A strange loop.

Sometime after Machu Picchu, where I sat sadly amidst cloudy stone staircases, scattered llamas, and empty rooms, I got sick.

Too many mosquito bites? The shower water I goofed and used to brush my teeth? Or perhaps that too-yellow chicken curry from the buggy outdoor market?

I didn't have enough left on my credit card to go to the hospital, so I shat and barfed quietly on repeat in the hostel room. I told the patient Diane to make our flight home without me—I couldn't abandon the bathroom or the bed. But she tucked me carefully into a taxi van instead, then pulled me out at the Cuzco airport. Mid-flight, bouncing through the misty mountaintops, I felt too close to a drifting, ethereal afterlife. After the flight attendant refused my panicked request for drop-down air, it occurred to me that I must start working much harder to be all right. I breathed slowly into Lima, where I tried again to eat, to drink water. Then went home.

Though Portland didn't necessarily feel like home.

Nowhere did.

From my dad's, I take the train to my best friend's wedding in Seattle. Her dress is like seawater, a deep, bright blue, with small flaps of fabric like a shimmering mermaid's tail. Her cake is ocean-themed. The groom is a little late. His vows are actually a poem that doesn't have much to do with any kind of promise, and the pair will later divorce. But he is happy now, and so is she, as are all the kilted groomsmen and black-suited bridesmaids, save me. I want to throw myself off the rooftop, but I can't ruin Gale's wedding. So I twist the corners of my mouth up and tighten my eyes into crinkles. There are no teeth in any of the event photos of me, but I am, indeed, observably smiling. I'm trying. And I *am* happy, for my friend.

Jonathan's birthday is the same day as the wedding. I take a groomsman to bed instead of calling him, and he texts me the next day, saying he thought he'd have heard from me.

But he doesn't want to leave L.A. to make a life with me elsewhere, and I'm not going back there.

So it might be time to leave one another alone.

I take the train home from Seattle, and everything looks the same out the window as it did going up.

Back at Dad's, I drag myself limply to the kitchen, then to the cabinet, open it, search out the Tylenol bottle. I shake it. Hold its fullness in my palm, breathing hard. Under my permanently-parched-seeming throat, my heart rings its insistence in my ears like a wild, common madness. I think of my dad, sitting there at work, calling clients and drawing equations. Eating lunch alone in his car, then a cigarette. Then pointing his clompy boots back past his officemates to his sales desk. They've nicknamed him the Jolly Boot Man, because he is so un-jolly in these boots. I think of my mom and brother, the newly married Gale, and brave Diane. I want to peel my brain from my body and fling it as far as my now sad-bony arms can manage. I want to take all these pills at once. But there's a heavy contract, in this equation, with the living, and they've labored far too long and too dearly to leave them hanging here.

So I will try again, I say, and command my hand to put the bottle back.

Sometimes I think time is shaped like an ouroboros: in self-destruction and simultaneous self-nourishment, contradictorily altering itself in order to maintain itself. Similarly, certain conspiracy theorists claim the earth's north and south poles are weakening, that when bipolarity fails, we'll see four or five magnetic "poles" split off from what we formerly thought could only be two. When dichotomy is devastated in this way, they say, earth's inhabitants will change by unknowable measure, but in some other ways, inevitably, remain themselves.

The magnet factory is just another kind of place, a microcosm in which to change and stay the same over time. Shifting my weight from foot to foot over the weeks, I discover that bald-topped Tom lives a simple life with his wife, who works at Walgreens. Talkative Candy, I learn, loves her little dog more than some people love their spouses. Joy can slip in at the seams. Repetitive work, the counting and packing of invisibly charged metals, can also illuminate: plodding, disciplined, I learn to trudge. When my mind wanders away beyond the factory floor—to lost love, regret, to the beauty of ten billion beckoning alternative potential life pathways—I can refocus. What is the goal today? To measure and wrap parts safely for travel.

To stabilize.

"How many grams is that?" asks Tom, in his quiet way. He points to the bag I'm scooping particles into. "Looks a little big. Maybe even it out."

Other Goals Besides Paying Attention: Get more sunshine. Be helpful. Earn enough money to look around the world again. Find a shapelier version of "stable."

It won't be as easy as a plane ticket.

It won't be instant insight.

And I won't be able to do it alone.

Yet it's not the hardest work there is: I'm not risking my fingers with rare-earth magnets or flying helicopters or spaceships made with them. I'm not pulling ore from a pit mine in Peru.

Maybe some other time, or in some other life, I'll have to.

A good teacher I had in Preskitt once told me that sometimes letting go of your own sorrow long enough to help someone else can accidentally initiate your own healing.

So I start a little reading-writing group, and from there a few of us members find companionship. It's not much, but it's something.

One night, just a few months before I will move back to Arizona, my dad catches me crying.

He reminds me about gratitude, about pulling things I need toward myself by allowing small graces to expand, giving them space and time.

He's right: I have a warm bed. A daily routine.

If nothing else, at this moment, I have a place to start, hopeful as the parched Atacama.

"I'm thankful for this warm bed," I repeat, tucking in, making mantra.

And the sound of rain above it.

The crashing sea.

The empty desert.

A softly shifting me.

Passage

1

Back in high school, my second job was easy: follow the servers out from the kitchen with the mobile metal condiment-carrier.

For each table with a tinfoil-wrapped baked potato, ask what toppings the potato eater desired.

If butter or sour cream, scoop up a ball and plop it down into the center of the presliced spud.

If chives or bacon bits, sprinkle liberally.

But I've always been clumsy. Often as not, I'd spill the ingredients meant to dress the spuds: butter balls projectiled onto blouses, bacon bits sprayed across skirts and chives confettied onto carpet. I once sloshed a whole pitcher of ice onto a brown-suited businessman trying to eke out the last bit of water from my pitcher into his glass.

I was scolded a lot, and when the owner, a mid-fifties-aged woman with green-shadowed eyelids and a bad beehive, mistakenly told me to stop flirting with the cooks and do my job—*they* had been flirting with *me*!—I was so fed up I told her I was taking a break, but instead strode out of the dimly lit steakhouse forever, chucking my waist apron in the dumpster.

In my car across the parking lot, I smoked an age-illegal cigarette, wondering what to do. How could I go home and tell my hard-working mom that I'd just quit my job like that?

I knew a lecture was forthcoming ("Walking without notice ruins resumes!"), but I wanted to be alone.

So I drove to the only place I knew, at age fifteen, to offer reprieve: the beach.

It was piss-raining, the Coast Range forest was full of dark twists, and the flickering headlights on my little 1983 hatchback worked about as well as my squeaky wipers. When I arrived, stressed out and nearly hypnotized from hearing the same single CD I had in the car on repeat for three hours, I stretched out of the car and called Mum.

Boy, was she miffed. She didn't even care about the job, as it happened. But apparently a teenager alone in another town at night smacked of trouble, even at a beach.

"There are all kinds of sickos out there," she exclaimed, "Besides, you have to be eighteen to rent a hotel room!"

Which I had not known.

So she read me her credit card number and told me to find a motel that would rent to me without ID.

I got to sleep by midnight, exhausted, wind howling around me in a creaky little mom-and-pop place right off the highway 101.

When I awoke, I scooted open the sliding glass door to an only barely blustery beach. A man and his golden retriever jogged silently down the surf, but there was no one else. Last night's storm had died down, the normal eerie early-morning fog had burned off, and as I stepped out toward the quiet, low waves kissing particulate creatures now scattered on the shore, I seemed to walk forever to reach the bubbling white line of seafoam. When my feet found the water, I took my shoes off and carried them, turning to walk along the shore until I couldn't see my room, or my car, or any other trappings of my normal half-functioning life.

2

My mom, a mental health counselor at that time, was and still is a big believer in the beach.

"It recalibrates people," she says. For years she wore an old blue sweatshirt that said, "I come to the sea to breathe." She and her sisters used to take me, my brother, and our cousins to the coast for family weekends, the only kind of therapy Mum really took for herself, after holding down coding patients in the hospital psych ward and watching a failing healthcare system shove the same patients from their hospital beds back to the streets until they returned again, mere weeks later.

We rented a family-style motel suite near rugged Cannon Beach a couple times, or one at the sandier Lincoln City, and sailed kites, rendered sand castles, or dug ourselves down into the wet hard-pack, pretending to get stuck. Every so often a few of us would get up the nerve to bolt out into the waves, then bounce around squealing in roiling knee-high water: a chilling proposition in Oregon any time of the year. Sometimes I could manage to stay out there awhile during summer, if I was with the braver Cousin Jason or intrepid Auntie Weez.

"It only takes two minutes, and then your legs go numb anyway," Auntie Weez said, and I agreed. It was the best place, out there, to watch seagulls, all the white wave caps and cloud streaks sparkling bright. Then we'd walk back to shore, knees wobbling, to towel off, squeak the ears and toe cracks clean of sand, and load into the car toward fresh fish dinner.

At this time, I adored the *Choose Your Own Adventure* volume where readers could transform into mermaids, swim down deep into dark sea trenches with the whales, and shed humanity: lose time, lose language.

The books always gave you choices to pick actions concordant with your comfort level at any given moment. Upon encountering the bottom of an ancient sailing vessel, which your fellow mermaid friend felt uneasy about, you could

    a. *Decide to swim up to it and climb aboard, and turn to page X.*

    b. *Decide to avoid contact with it and swim with your friend toward a familiar island instead, turning to page Y.*

Of course, I delighted in these imaginings: the falling away of routine daily things I had to do, like school, turning instead to the freedom implicit in mystery. At fourteen, at Cape Cod, I swam out past my brother, past the breakers, until I couldn't hear my dad and his new girlfriend arguing on the shore anymore, and I wasn't scared. At nineteen I clambered, with companions or alone, out onto Pacific City's secret sandstone bluffs, up the megadune of sliding sand granules, and past the skimpy tsunami warning sign attached to a scant wire fence. Venturing out into the private wonderland there, past windswept trees twisted in miniature, tide pools tucked full of oysters and anemones, I reached the end of the peninsula. Surrounded almost 360 degrees by sea, one can feel starkly a part of the still-wild world, yet apart from its dangers: salt spray that would spatter your skin, wind that would shove you, and weighted waters pounding into rocks and coves below. Gray whales rise to spout on their way south, breaking the hard, flat line between slate sea and feathered sky.

3

My mother, I've always thought, is a pretty adventurous and adaptable person. Born conveniently for my imperfect memory in the exact middle of the last century, 1950, to a U.S. Air Force family, she'd lived in London by age six, Turkey by eight. One of her first precollege jobs was packing veggies at a cannery in Eastern Oregon, though later she would hang around the famous fish cannery row of Steinbeck's novels in Monterey. Before becoming a Russian linguist there, she played violin in the Seattle Symphony and danced ballet. She rafted the Colorado through the Grand Canyon long before I relocated to its gaping mouth myself. Freshly divorced in her forties, she took a quiet trip to Ireland with a lover (then another trip, to Egypt, with another). On my desk I still keep a picture of her cross-legged on a camel, the Sphinx rising from the rolling sand behind her.

While my dad told me I should have been a computer programmer ("Just like that poetry you love," he said, bless his heart), Mum always told me I could do whatever I actually wanted to do for work. She herself had a pretty interesting job, helping people's states of mind, assuring the mentally unstable that they had a place in this world and that, with the right personalized formulas of habit and health, they could be happy here.

"What do *you* want to do?" she asked, perched on the edge of my bed one day, where I'd had a mid-teenage meltdown.

I sighed, throwing my hands in the air. "I just want to live an extraordinary life."

I didn't learn, until adulthood, many of the extraordinary mysteries of my mother's life, which perhaps contributed to her grit, her resilience, and her ability to pluck patience during duress from some deeply private place inside herself. Before she was a counselor and a mother, my mother met my father in the army, translating Russian from the radio on a mountaintop compound in Germany. Before that, she'd taken intelligence and language training in California, one of nine cadets to pass from an incoming class of forty-two.

In Carmel, where I road-tripped with a cheaterly ex-boyfriend, I remembered this. Our first day there, at the famous marine center, I got to see, up close and daylit, the slimy variety of strange creatures that slid beside me, unnoticed, in the gray coastal waters of the Pacific. Afterward my ex and I threw frisbees on the beach with his stepmom, then we all shared a suddenly spooky seafood lunch. On the way home we passed the sign for the military language school, and I recalled how hard my mom had worked to pass classes most other people in her unit couldn't hack. Here she'd been engaged to marry a different man than my dad: Happy, a Marine, a black man at a time when white women like Mum weren't supposed to date them, a kind karate master and scuba enthusiast. I found his framed picture tissue-wrapped in my childhood closet, and when I first asked her about it, she cried. Years later I asked her again, and got a long e-mail. It ended this way:

One morning Happy was going to go diving with his buddy, Dave. He changed his mind the night before because the weather was bad, which would make the diving more dangerous. Then, the next morning, Dave called and said, "I think the weather's ok, let's go diving anyway." So they did.

He drowned that day, October 22, 1973, Butterfly Beach.

Years after Happy's death, and recently divorced from my dad, Mum slept on the couch of our two-bedroom apartment in small-town Kentucky, where she'd given my brother and me each one of the two total bedrooms. She was a newly minted mental-health counselor then, now single and middle-aged, trying to move us back toward her family in Oregon, broke, and involved in a tricky court dispute over child support.

Things were hard, looked bleak, and she was tired.

One morning, she said, she woke up to the distinct feeling of Happy's hand on her lower back: his presence, it seemed, offering relief, assuring her she'd be all right.

And after that, somehow, she was.

4

One day, aged twenty, living in Portland not far from the sea but too busy to go anymore, I realized my period was late. I was living with a different former boyfriend, whom I loved but who, I knew, should be with someone else: someone who wanted to make a stable home in Portland, rock-climb and snowboard. Selfish, I still sought to see the world. No submersion into the world of uterine mystery. I didn't want to drown in diapers. Half timid and half intrepid, I ached, instead, to choose adventure.

"Do you want to have it?" Niles asked, when I said I was late.

a. *If you choose to be stable, do nothing.*

"I don't know," I said, but I did.

b. *If you choose more freedom, find a clinic.*

"Well—" he took my hand "—it's your choice."

By the time, a few days later, I finally nerved up to admit that I wanted an abortion and went to tell Niles, my period suddenly started. So we began discussing better birth control.

5

When she was young, years before she labored for me, my mother had accidentally gotten pregnant. Her early-model IUD hurt, so she'd had it removed, then . . . oops.

The local late-1960s doctors she consulted didn't think she "looked sad enough" for an abortion and wouldn't offer it.

So it was that my grandma, Mum's mom, who herself loved children and who'd once been told by a different batch of doctors that her uterus would never support an embryo, flew with my mom to Japan for a procedure to remove one, and cared for her afterward.

When I asked Mum (who, unsurprisingly, didn't sell me on an IUD) for a more permanent form of contraception, she called around and found the only place in town that would help a twenty-year-old woman with no previous children to remain child-free: an abortion clinic.

She set an appointment. Took me down for the mandatory counseling session, where they believed me when I told them I wouldn't change my mind about not wanting kids and sue. They explained how, instead of the cutting and cauterizing version of old-time tubals, doctors now would take two tiny rubber bands to the fallopian tubes, bend a little elbow in the tissue of the tunnels, and compress each one, much like cutting off water to a yard hose. That way, the mother's egg, too large to fit through, waits at the bend until it dies and reabsorbs into her tissue, while the hormones needed for maintenance of the would-be mother's own body can continue flowing.

A week later I came safely home after the drug-induced nap during which these crimp-bands were set in place. What I didn't realize, in my postoperative grogginess, or until years later with a more nuanced understanding of American healthcare, was that it had been considered an elective procedure and therefore not actually "covered," as Mum had told me, by her insurance. She'd paid for it secretly out of her own slim salary.

6

The last time, in my twenties, that I plunged into the dark Pacific waves I used to love, my heart skipped and threatened, I thought, to stop from the shock of the cold. Another time, I was bowled over by a sneaker wave, pulled outward; I came up sputtering and gasping mid-seascape to struggle, panicked, back to safety. In Hawaii on our honeymoon, my now-spouse Tim had to lure me into the mostly placid little bay near our room (a rum drink helped) to snorkel, even just with some friendly local sea turtles. While the ancient slow-flapping disc-creatures delighted, I squawked at every sand swirl on the seabed, conjuring menace, then sucking salt water into my scuba mask.

Maybe it was too much *Shark Week*. Or Fukushima. Hurricane Katrina. Or Sandy, which my brother lived through in New York, skirting subway tunnels suddenly waterlogged. Whatever it was, when the surf came in far and deep one bright Hawaiian day, a rare "king tide," I watched Tim body-surf the froth in horror, watched him laugh like a child as the waves shot him farther and harder into the shore each time, rolled him over and pummeled him.

Maybe, as I've aged, I ponder now, I've become more reticent in general: the cloak of youthful invincibility stripped from my shoulders by years of successive risk and recovery. I cling to rocks I used to leap from. When I go to the seaside now, I scan the horizon as I slather on the sunscreen, eyes searching out the distant line, the incoming wall of water I just know, in these climate-changing times, could thunder in to crush and pull me tumbling back from all the human experience I hold tight to: light, solid footing, atmospheric oxygen, and a comfortable spot at the top of the food chain.

When I dream of the tropics now, I'm on a ship: it is sinking.

I'm on an old worn-out high-rise building: it's flooding.

When I tiptoe into tidewaters, quick and unstable, I understand how my mom must be braver than me, returning again and again to the place that pulled her first beloved fiancé from her and into its own wet depth. I, meanwhile, escape to places free of mystery now. I close cavern doors. Seal secret chambers. Shine evaporative sunlight onto tide pools and fill in tunnels with bright, dry sand, landbound. Somehow, some way, I've grown more appreciative of what I see than what I can't. Maybe it's aging. But maybe it's something else.

"The opposite of love is fear," some of mom's old counseling books have mentioned, as I've thumbed through them, belly-down on carpet. "When you let go of fear, you can love."

When I'm at my most fearful, though, I think its opposite is joy.

When I'm not afraid, I feel easy, whether I feel loved or not.

But I suppose none of these emotions are opposites, spread apart and pushing this way or that. They seem, rather, bound as in the vertical axis of an iceberg, visible beauty conjoined with risk below.

7

In Wupatki, Arizona, a ruins-made-state-park, you can walk among old rocks and find trilobites: sea creatures curled into statis when ancient salt water compressed and then abandoned old sediment. There's an ancient volcano there, too: Sunset Crater, a moonscape of sharp black lava hardened into hole-riddled sponge stone. If you pick up a piece, you'll find it eerily lightweight: a little bit of burden that you expected to carry, lifted. When I consider Wupatki, I ponder the opposites there, how desert and sea traded places once.

If you drive south from Wupatki down past Phoenix, then Tucson, then not far into Mexico, the desert head-butts the sea. There's no tropical transition, no forested fade between inland earth and deep sapphire Sea of Cortez. One year in Arizona, I got to go there, to the old tourist haven at this interface: to live the American Dream of vacating America for a place we once forayed into, and now are building a wall against, but want to go back again to visit when we feel like it: Mexico. This opportunity came because my bosses and friends, more financially solvent than me, owned a time-share, and my pal Lindsay and I were invited to join them. We planned to write a business plan there, brainstorm arts resource ideas between swimming and exploring, storytelling and relaxing.

We all drove south together, crossed the border easily, and saw the line snaking back in the other direction, clogged at the gate. Off the dusty highway, we watched daily work commence in the crumbling streets of the town: locals trudging through slicing heat with bushels on their burros, thick fabric sacks on their own backs. They wrenched on beat-up old pickup trucks roadside, waved flies from fresh fruit stands, passed paper-wrapped tortillas through house side-door windows. We passed a small stadium built for bullfighting and, my boss said, bare-knuckle boxing. We passed police armed with semiautomatics adjusting their riot gear, and semi-vacant hotel developments left over and looming, the plywood-boarded but still colorful nightclubs abandoned after a notorious 1980s cartel killing spree.

Then we dined at the Friendly Dolphin, full of old celebrity photos, still serving ceviche in huge bowls in huge rooms, but to what I'd imagine was less than a quarter of its former clientele. We drank crushed-ice cocktails on the back balcony overlooking a bay, ate too many tacos, and overtipped, embarrassed at the restaurant's emptiness. Then we finally approached the compound where Americans go to winter, a crop of not-quite-cookie-cutter Grecian-style faux adobe mansions, mostly pink or white, clustered beyond the long yellow-tan sand with its scorpions, spiders, and bleached-out bones of dubious identity unfurling outward for miles. Catholic schoolgirls in knee-length skirts streamed slowly from a painted-concrete box, then started, on foot, to cross the dunes. Not far past them, at the gates of American expat splendor, a uniformed guard waved us in, and the girls disappeared into the dust.

In the house there was beauty: one room connected to the next with casual half-walls and open showers, boundaries between spaces calmed by consistently inlaid mosaic counters and pleasing slick Saltillo, forming slow sound-flow past windows and doors cut to comforting roundness in the corners.

These portals led out to the line where a flat blue panel of reflection lay still, as if waiting, under a bright, wide sky. Once we'd settled, we dragged plastic chairs down to it. We were safe, but local vendors, suntanned and barefoot, were approaching, selling jewelry, massage. Their survival: tenuous.

More desperation ensued in the sea: sardines swept squirming into the tide, and long-necked pelicans plummeting straight through its surface to pop up gulping. We bumbled into kayaks and paddled outward, where, under the rippling water, I spied a small shark. Or was it a ray? My pulse began to race at every passing shadow.

My pal Lindsay, of the business plan, paddled faster than me, her technique perfected in years of guiding Grand Canyon river trips. I wobbled as I paddled, pausing every few feet for balance. I corrected my route right, then left, felt my skin singeing in the sun as my speedy friend grew smaller.

To my left now: a heaving, swelling blue blanket.

To my right: a momentary home surrounded by seashells and succulents.

Me, in the middle, afraid on the waves.

I thought of Mum, her trip to the Grand Canyon. The photo of her shows brown hair, short and wild, curling back as the crowded eight-person raft they all clung to tipped downward into foam. Her sunglasses on, I could never see trepidation, or lack thereof, although where she was, mid-river, I guess it wouldn't have mattered.

I gave up on paddling for a moment and let the tide take me. My untrained arms ached.

My untrained arms ached, but I could smell things I imagined to be new to me. I saw parts of otherworldly beings poke occasionally skyward from soft chop: creatures nosing newness, tentative.

Creatures I imagined to be free. Or mostly so.

What was it I feared? Underwater sea suction? Caves or tunnels? Great slimy beasts coming up from the deep, not just for air, but for me? Did it matter?

In the kayak, waves thumping in echo against the hull, the existential jammed into the practical.

a. *If you choose to head home, wrench your boat around to face the shore.*

b. *If you choose to stay out here with Lindsay, understand you'll have to paddle faster. Or you'll simply drift away.*

Either choice required effort.

8

Once, a major relationship of mine was failing; my lover, the one I went to Carmel with, leaned toward free love.

I didn't, being scared too constantly of love-theft, but still, I feared to lose him outright. So I tried to share.

Every other woman's glance was a risk; every outing skirted danger. The future felt unknowable, as his draw to the new both exhilarated and annihilated.

I had a nightmare not long before we split.

In it, I was sprinting away from a hard-faced man who looked like a generic James Bond movie character. He ran fast after me, doubling down through twisting stairwells of a giant old house, down its dark, narrow halls.

He meant to catch me. I meant to live another day.

Out onto the rain-slick roof I burst.

Over its edge I glimpsed the grimy river below, swamp-green with detritus.

It seemed my last chance, and I doubted he'd follow, so I leapt.

But a second after, I found myself underwater, and he landed too, plunging in beside me in a sharp blast of bubbles. I felt his rough hand on my ankle, then my waist.

He would drown me, I knew.

But instead the stranger wrapped his arms around me like a lover, drew me close, and kissed me. As he did, all my air escaped. And yet, as I watched the bubbles rise away, I realized I could still breathe.

The man let me go, smiled, swam away, and I was left underwater, alone, in new mystery. I could see, for the first time, at close range, beauty in the grime of submersion: Algae. Dim-lit life. It felt like I spent hours underwater there, breathing.

And then I awoke, unafraid.

Osmosis

1

Route 66.

Train tracks.

An old but still functional Amtrak route delivers a long chain of containers through the center of town, two-directionally, twice a day—once in the morning and once at 9 p.m.—stopping there for about an hour, which jams traffic up to a mile out while it unloads passengers into nearby hotels and bars, whisking others off eastward or westward. Other trains don't carry people, just cargo, and they don't stop.

Here's the train now. Two striped and blinking arms lower, and I wait with an accumulating throng of returning-home bargoers amidst the warning bells for the mammoth machine to pass. No one tries to sprint across and "beat the train" this time, and I sigh, relieved: every few months, a drunk-brave and impatient college student, or a suicidal depressive, will self-crush vis-à-vis the fast-moving freighters barreling through town. These freighters move too fast to stop quickly for track impediments, even when the screeching brakes are thrown. Especially since the engines stopped blowing their horns within city limits (a tourist accommodation, I have heard), sometimes potential track-crossers can't tell how close incoming danger really is. My first month in town, a tipsy woman twirling near the train tracks in a luscious red dress and fur coat had twirled too close to a coming engine. Snow burst up, scenically, magically, from the tracks. About the time I'd decided to warn her of her proximity, a metal ladder on one of the cars hooked her arm and slapped her fast onto the pavement. She didn't die, but she left in the ambulance I called. Two days later, police appeared at my door with my subpoena: the railway wanted to nail her for trespassing.

About two years later, on my way to a meeting downtown, I stretched my neck up over a crowd of jamming car- and foot-traffic to find: just a pale leg twisted the wrong way beneath a lump of flannel, closely guarded by EMTs. I forgot where I'd been going and diverted to a local bar immediately for a stiff drink. The township imagines a bridge or tunnel that could divert the flow of human forms more safely across the tracks, but as yet no one's made real plans to build one.

Even if we don't get "trained," for folks who live here permanently—who hike, take in concerts, cook scratch-made whole-food meals, meditate, visit vortexes, make soap, assemble jewelry, build yurts, or read in coffee shops rather than climbing a well-paying professional ladder—the feeling of being overrun creeps consistently. Flagstaff follows the tragic housing tradition of the West: unscrupulous developers, stretching highway sprawl, cookie-cutter condos, and student rentals with monthly rates rising sky-high. Flagstaff's basic infrastructure wasn't created to accommodate the now-booming university student and tourist populations. Although, I suppose, you could say the strange crashing together of fast growth and slow small-town cultures feels interesting.

In grad school I'd gone with a friend from Flagstaff out old Route 66 to Winslow. He was sad, apart from his partner that year, and I was aimless, so we drove to see what the Eagles song discussed: how to take it easy on a highway with attractive people in flatbed Fords who might stare at us. When we got there, it was empty. Most buildings were burned out or boarded up, and the ones that weren't seemed lonely. I recall that we'd had plans for lunch but only stopped to buy gas and a long strip of lotto tickets on our way back to our busier town, with its weird old motels and sun-buzzed, ten-block-big downtown. Flagstaff's not really a town for people seeking fame or fortune, at least not yet, but it has energy. And also:

Clean air and a nice strong sun but without, at high altitude, high heat.

Hiking for miles.

Food for fad diets.

A plethora of outdoor seating that encourages lounging in the mostly bug-free, crystalline-azure-skied paradise.

Don't forget the giant otherworldly ravens that hop like miniature people from street to picnic table, company for the semipermanent all-weather patio barflies, the often familiar homeless faces, the anarchist house-show punks and train kids, the oddball small-town lawyers and real estate mini-moguls.

Here loyalties build over time, simply as one sees the same folks repeatedly, and all you have to do to be liked, generally speaking, is show up and not be a dick. People share gossip, hobbies, and lovers: and since you can't avoid seeing anyone for too long, you learn to play nice, be mostly symbiotic.

2

That first winter I arrived, it snowed more in Flag than it did in Anchorage, Alaska. You could go to a little bridge near the college, the kind that crosses over a drainage creek, and jump into powder up to your head. For the first time in my life, I had an office: I was a GTA, teaching for tuition, and the space was shared, but still, I could sleep there while I looked for housing, which I did, the kindly janitors I got to know by name ignoring me when they came in, early mornings, to check the trash.

My first room after that was $350, all included. I ached and sweated my way through swine flu there. I dated a friend of my colleague: a canyoneer. We'd all drive up the highway to Zion, in Utah. We zipped into dry suits (warmer big-brothers to wetsuits) and waded through chilly slot canyons, where I learned how quickly sun and shade can change your experience of reality.

We rappelled down smooth rock walls, just like in the army.

One hike we took, just me and this boyfriend, we got lost, missed a mini-cairn of stacked rocks meant to mark the path, and found ourselves scrambling up the side of a nearly-sheer cliff. The boyfriend, a climber as well as a canyoneer, was confident. Myself, merely a follower into this land: I was not.

"If we get out of this," I said to whatever people think is listening when they beg non-people for help, "I'll never blindly follow a man again." I promised I'd finally learn boundaries.

And we got out.

When my awesome cheap room was revoked for remodeling (read: rent raise), I moved into a new complex that my new roommate and I dubbed Grey Gardens because of the sea of impenetrable parking around it, and because of our old landlady, a terrifying evangelical who said Halloween led people to hell.

Roomie Rachel and I were both recently emerged from failed long relationships, and it was cold that winter, so we distracted ourselves from school life with whiskey sipping, late-night storytelling, and dancing. We'd walk over to meet our pals Tiny Professor and Sonni and swirl around the local concrete club floor, arms outstretched like airplanes. Sonni, a B-boy, impressed us with his pop locks. Tiny Prof, who could play guitar behind her back, could spin like "Stand Back" Stevie Nicks without dropping over from dizziness.

You could hear it from the street outside:
Dirty bass.
Tasty bass.
Crunchy bass.
Nasty bass.
Salty bass.
Sexy bass.
Cosmic bass.

There are myriad ways to describe EDM (Electronic Dance Music, or Tronic) in wild synesthesia, the senses crossing, then crushing together.

As you draw close to the stage, muted thuds get crisper, deeper. Pretty soon, especially after a drink, both melody and bass are laid loud upon your body. Into your stomach, your shoulders. Your head bobs on its own.

There are many reasons to seek it out, even if, like me, you're new to the scene. Maybe it's a late night after work, and you want to move in a nonmechanical way again.

Or you're blue.

Lovelorn.

Fucked up about finances.

Or tired of being tired.

Maybe you want to move because you're nervous.

You need to feel alive again.

You're cold.

Or, you don't want to dance, but your pals have dragged you there.

You ache to be joined in mass friendship.

I remember something my dad said once about the army, when I complained of the running regime I'd experienced there:

"It's like being part of a bigger body," he'd said. "You don't even exist anymore, when you all march together." He had enjoyed that synthesis.

And this EDM thing was similar, but with no cadences on killing, just a feeling of dissolve and then a bonding. The bass crawls up your spine. You all sway in concert. If you sit on the subwoofer near the stage—almost as tall as Tiny Prof herself—the top of your head will vibrate and you will think that maybe it's the universe talking.

"House music mimics the four-four timing of the beating human heart," the shaggy neo-hippy by the back door expounded, patting his chest in a steady mini-demo. Past him, Sonni the B-boy flipped onto his back, then spun, legs skyward.

"People can do that?" I gasped. But then, we didn't seem like units of "people."

We were melded into "person" by motion.

Sonni and I were just cells.

3

I was beginning to nurture a feeling, born of such bone-cold winter nights, now made liquid, that if I stopped overthinking and pontificating, left my academic training behind awhile and listened, this new activity could weasel into me and change me into something I could never have predicted.

In school, I was meant to Argue. Analyze. Devise.

I was meant to speak with authority while teaching, especially about how to argue, analyze, and devise.

At bars after classes, creative writing colleagues and I, lovably more lax than our lit major counterparts, waxed poetic on famous poets, other programs, places to publish. We badmouthed bad students and flailed around about fixing failing pedagogy.

But the club scene went elsewhere. None of the stress mattered here, where a woman slid down red silk, suspended in ribbons from thick ceiling beams. Where three others spun blinking neon hoops in unison. Behind them all, ambient video swirled slowly across giant fabric screens, and wandering spotlights filtered up like pink snow through the darkness of the crowd, peppering our faces in flashes. There was no more me talking. Every time I showed up outside the halls of higher knowledge, descended into these darkened downtown bowels, people at last began to blend effortlessly, and I with them.

No hierarchy.

No status.

In this new kind of communitas, my worries about "making it," about the need to distinguish myself in some way for my survival, were extinguished.

Flagstaff: a place of plenty in dance-party options. Zombie Prom, Electric Kingdom, Ladies' 80s, the S&M Ball. For a town of only 75,000, give or take student influx/outflow, there was great hunger and zeal for bass magic. So, after my gratifying but not-financially-game-changing graduate degree, I considered seriously whether to stick around. Daytime Flagstaff reminded me of remnants of my less-than-fantastic high school tenure in Oregon: old leftover logging culture, old settler spirit, dark foliage, and slushy, slippery February streets. I thought it had a dumb name too: named for a pole with a flag on it. This seemed a subtle reminder that prior to said flag, the region was occupied by indigenous tribes who hadn't had to use flags to stake such claims. At least twelve native peoples still call the mountain peaks home, rising like cathedrals before the Painted Desert, their sacred space. They, and some of the more conscious newcomers, protest the constant purchase, sale, and development of the highest one, Humphreys Peak, as ski resort fun for those wealthy Phoenicians and Californians yearning for a quick taste of winter. On Humphreys's Snowbowl resort, snowblowers now spray greywater powder over slopes that people in the know hesitate to ski. One acquaintance climbed a tree in protest of it and sat there until he was arrested.

Since I didn't have another Big New Goal, I decided to stick around for this unfolding of the times. Twenty-eight, freshly freed and degreed, fairly fit and healthy, and ready to relax into a new hometown, I knew my sense of history about the Southwest needed updating. I'd always felt squashed chasing culture in big cities, but I'd heard there was strong artsy stuff in town here, though I'd been too busy writing papers to notice. So I would, I decided, stay.

But where would I work? The rising cost of living dictated I would have several jobs. I would teach a smattering of adjunct English courses. Sometimes bartend. Eventually run an open mic. Then a bingo night. A trivia night. Work front desk at a hostel, then live there too, to save on rent.

So when you think of a hostel, what do you conjure?

The word "hostel" connotes a different kind of place than the better-known worldwide establishment for travel accommodation, the hotel: hostels are more casual, more communal, and follow the roots of the old European tradition of promoting outdoor activity and stewardship, with many of our guests arriving to hike or boat the Colorado River.

Sometimes people think hostels are dirty, reliant in their early days upon lackadaisical guests pitching in to tidy; but ours wasn't, because our staff actually cleaned it. Cleaned *them*, I should say. Built in the late 1800s, one building contained two floors of old wooden rooms, two kitchens, five detached bathrooms, and a small concrete smoking patio. It and a nearby 1929 motorcourt were owned by the same married couple.

Lina, our main boss and half of this husband-wife team, was always very neat, and since she always asked nicely ("Would you mind giving the banister a little extra attention today?"), I was happy to aid in this effort. Although I hadn't thought I'd grow up to be a housecleaner, I found I relished the work, especially its quiet meditative moments, after the majority of guests were out for the day or tucked away at night. I made my way around the property, stripping sheets, washing dishes, dusting, turning lights on or dimming them for mood, scrubbing toilets, or, my favorite, watering plants. Not long after I was hired as a cleaner, one of the front desk clerks was threatened by a guest and quit on the spot. Then I got a promotion.

I got a better room: it was yellow.

I got to check people in and out, and tell them all I knew about the area, which at first was not much: how to get to the Grand Canyon, where to go in town for food. Eventually my knowledge grew and I knew which specific paths to hike. How to apply for backcountry permits. That Meteor Crater had no obvious alien activity. Whether Winslow was really worth a stop (it's not).

Being a "deskie," over time, somehow proved simultaneously interesting and dull. Oftentimes guests, oftentimes men who cornered me counting money, would stop to lob the Standard Three Queries at me:

1. "Where are you from?"
2. "How long have you been here?"
3. "So, are you a student?"

When they found I was a teacher instead, many grew more careful manners, but the conversations were still redundant. And oftentimes, usually on late shift, duties segued into shushing loud guests and preventing fights or fires: also repetitive. By virtue of our cheap shared dorm beds, we attracted, in addition to well-meaning but bedbug-bearing hikers: drunk Europeans, drunk Aussies, drunk American unhoused folks, the deeply mentally ill, burned-out aggro Route 66 bikers, and plenty of drug-obsessed hippies.

People got rowdy.

Kitchens got crowded.

And I got tired, gulping cold stale breakfast coffee to keep myself alert.

"Let me paint you this picture," I'd say when I trained incoming deskies, shaping my hands around an invisible sphere. "We (deskies) are like an osmotic membrane: equalizing the concentration of people inside and outside the hostel. We let the congenial guests in, and keep troublemakers out."

And although most guests I'd experienced were "net neutral," I would tell them, it was better to err on the side of not checking someone in than to figure out how to eject that same someone later.

Like Fake Pregnant Woman.

Energy Vampire.

Loud Sex French Lesbians (screwing in a shared dorm room).

New Employee Meth Binger.

Thief With Fake Cast!!!

Box Cutter Threatener (the cops came just in time).

Furious Smoky Steak Cooker (turned Obsessive, Obscene Prank Caller).

And of course: Innovative Room 12 Poop Wall Decorator.

Jonny Escalante, one of my favorite coworkers, left sticky notes on the computer: "Two douchebag jizzbags (Whoever and Fairydust) think they can harass our cleaning staff . . . and they play bad guitar: No Fly."

Part of my job was to go into the database and update our No-Fly list, people we would no longer check in again, which scrolled extensively by the end of my six-year tenure, such that a brand-new deskie wouldn't actually feasibly have time to read it upon checking someone new (to them) in.

Jonny—tall, lanky, with fierce resting underbite—was the most intimidating deskie. Big sneer. Sweet friend, though: he fiddled with a guitar in the lobby and told me of his hometown, Nogales, and of being a grip for small movies for his almost-finished film degree, and of his dad being stuck by lightening, twice.

Coworkers become a created and necessary new family. When Jonny Escalante's aunt came to tell him, mid-shift, that his mother had suddenly died, Lina's husband and co-owner told Jonny he himself would cover all future missed shifts, for as long as he needed, offered him money, and sent him from the desk to go immediately home with his aunt.

When I had a risky eye surgery, it was my friend Syd, and Ricardo and Annie, two coworkers living in the attic as a couple, who came to hold my hand, bring me food, and help me dial the after-care nurse when my vision took on a hell-colored tinge in the middle of a hostel holiday party.

There was Mark, our monklike sixty-something who lived in the other half of the attic and healed our headaches with pressure-point pinching.

Lucky Louie, a soapmaker, trail runner, and now canyon guide from Ohio, who was almost eaten by mountain lions once, then another time thrown from a motorbike. We started a weekly juice and cooking club together.

Enter Daniel, now an engineering student who'd recovered from some rough time living in the gritty San Francisco streets.

And Sal, the hostel owners' son, with whom I began a tiny grassroots arts exchange time-share on hostel grounds.

So many others, come and gone.

We gossiped, talked shop: about the tour van stolen, then found empty and abandoned in Tuba City, about guests we'd had romantic intrigue with, about coworkers smoking weed on the job and then losing their jobs. When deskies went dancing or pool-playing together, the storytelling gallows humor was rivaled by none. One year I even borrowed money to buy the cheapest three acres of land then listed in Arizona with Lucky Louie. We envisioned living there, forty minutes out of town, in next-door tiny homes, and eventually, although I moved away, he built one, and lives there.

It was fun. But would it last?

I began to ask myself:

How many beds can you make in an hour for entitled tourists before you begin to hope they fall into a canyon?

How many times can you corral floating turds from overflowed toilets before you wish them freedom, and yourself besides?

For how many hours, days, and weeks in a row?

I thought sometimes of quitting in search of a more "normal" job. Perhaps one with more straightforward clients, and a workforce accountable to an up-to-date H.R. department. Parts of me, I could sense, were becoming hard. I turned away a legless vet in a wheelchair once, just minutes after closing, despite his begging for a bed: I felt he might be unstable, and I had a mission to "protect" the hostel community and its guests.

But it was fucking snowing.

The emotional and moral toll could pile up. But I couldn't quite quit: not yet. There were also little humanizing perks of intangible but somehow high value:

The hostel threw holiday parties where, often, all the food provided by Lina was homemade.

I wore any comfortable clothing I wanted.

I never had to work mornings.

Workers got surprise raises without having to ask for them and, if the business did particularly well, a bonus at the end of the summer high season.

And if disaster happened, Lina pulled staffers aside, discreetly, to describe a mistake. I found it refreshingly personal after some corporate jobs I'd had, and it must have worked for others too: most staffers stayed, and aimed to please.

We treated guests well and befriended many.

Faith was one of these friends. She came from Great Britain but sought medical care and a new life here in the hills. She'd had a wild life once, nearly dying from food allergies and abused by her caretakers. She came on a work exchange and eventually acquired a student visa. Something she told me stays with me: that there's a strange kind of safety in exposure, the public environment of the hostel community, where it's hard to hide illness, sorrow, and bad behavior. "Home" for her, here, had become not simply a place to watch TV after work and to sleep, but also a protected space in which to talk, earn a bed, learn, share, and work together at understanding the mystery of human happiness.

Once, there was a visitor whose name I've forgotten. Like many of our visitors, he was stranded temporarily because his car broke down, just as if Flagstaff had sucked him into its vortex and didn't want to let him go. While he waited some weeks for a needed but obscure car part to arrive at the repair shop, he played guitar and talked with us all about books and wanderlust. When I asked where he was wandering next, he told me: Idaho, though where he really wanted to go was Montana.

"Then why not go to Montana?" I asked. It was summer, the best time of year in Big Sky country.

He told me he'd built it up too much in his mind. Montana: land of space, wildflowers, and silence.

"What if it didn't live up?" he asked. Then the most monumental of his dreams would be dashed.

He'd go as close as Idaho, he said, and leave the dream to exist, free and unharmed from a safer distance: still reachable, like a pack of cigarettes you know you keep in the freezer, but which you dare not open, lest you run out.

4

On one Ladies' 80s Wednesday, a man I'd never seen before had perched on the edge of the stage, facing away from the DJ and in toward the dancers but looking down, just rolling a smoke as if he were the only person in the room. It's funny, in hindsight, the cinematic way the crowd of dancers shifted at this moment to create a kind of aisle, perfectly pointing me to see him from the bar: glasses, navy peacoat. Black turtleneck. Short, fuzzy beard.

"My glasses!" I heard him exclaim, in the same moment I saw the lenses glint from the floor near the base of the stage. I beelined over the glitter-sprayed concrete, bent down before him, then tucked the frames back into his hand, and he looked at me like I was a miracle.

Fate is fast, I've long felt, and small: it zips along, paperclip-sized. In the miniature moment he said thank you, I knew that I would date him. The first time he came over to my house, we cuddled. The smell of him, pungent and earthy without deodorant, intoxicated in the same way as his disregard for all the things I'd previously thought were important. Like conformity. Prestige. Even basic stability.

Aiden was a DJ, a music producer, as he called it: he made beep-boop sounds on his computer. He wrote poetry and liked to dance. He wanted to travel, he said, much like I did, and we both seemed to value creativity more than most other qualities.

There were, of course, things we didn't like about each other:

He stole groceries. I spent too much.

He didn't vote. I didn't pay enough attention to politics, but voted anyway.

He'd let his student loan debt lapse into default, and he'd never be able to use conventional credit. I could, but I had more student debt than God.

He sold party drugs. I worried about him getting busted. He thought I was prude.

Yet he offered me new kinds of value, showing me what self-care was. Unlike me, he didn't have to plan each day. We could walk downtown for breakfast, run into a friend, decide to take a hike. Then maybe come home and nap, or work on a low-pressure afternoon project just for fun: cook up some soup, rearrange a garden, pen a lazy song or plan a party. He demonstrated yoga stretches to relieve the aching "vulture neck" I acquired from hunching, workbound, over my laptop. He poked at pressure points in my feet when I stood too long at the hostel front desk.

And his friend group, which was enormous, exposed me to some odd, sometimes fun new ideas: conspiracy theories of alternate human histories, numerology, chakras, ancient aliens, aural energy.

Did you know, they said, that fluoride shrinks your pineal "third eye" gland, quasi-collapsing your connection to the divine? I didn't!

Did you know, said another, that Jesus was actually . . . a mushroom?

One of Aiden's besties, a wild-eyed kind of local guru, explained that animals who die for human meat meals create "pain food," their terror still swelling through their flesh after death: not good to ingest into your own tissue—and reason enough to be vegan. We are all connected, he said, whether we want to be or not.

Which might be how Aiden's ideology of polyamory also thrived: at night he performed at local house parties while I, often sleepy by midnight, would try to stay awake until the end. If I didn't, I feared he would leave with other ladies, and these fears were not absurd. Once, I watched him play at a smoky Halloween party, joint in hand, sweaty glasses foggy, while he pushed his controller buttons and twisted his knobs, elbowing a perfectly flat and undanceable song into a heavy bass mashup I never would have thought could work. When the new big beat fell into just the right moment and married the motions of two separate songs together, the room exploded into crazed and unexpected unison. How my heart swelled for him. How did everyone's.

It was lovemaking. It was climax. It was cuddle time. I was lucky when it occurred with me.

The ethos of the festi-kids—for I don't know what else to call them—is generally "love-oriented," left over from the sixties, and as such is generally pacifist, in philosophy if not in practice. Compared to some social groups I've encountered (like rednecks, jocks, or academics), festi-kids don't seem to fight that much, and when they do encounter conflict, reconciliation is actively sought with a variety of self-help and socially mediated tools. Self-soothing remedies—sound healing or smell therapy, meditation or massage—could calm one back down into balance. Then one could address communal issues through interventions, small group meetings, or moon-cycle ceremonies incorporating prayers to whatever deity one chose. The goal: to heal, reconnect. As a general mediating type of a person, I understood.

Of course, there are problems with certain of their practices, even if the festi-kids might not cop to them. They may not like guns, meat, or the pantomimed violence of most team sports, but they still compete in subtle ways, managing to maim each other by mostly emotional methods. Hierarchy, unclear on darkened dance floors, springs forth again in daylit displays of an almost competitive "goodness" or "health." Whose waistline wears best, indicating dietary discipline, a pinned-on festival foxtail? Whose skin is most luminous, because they invest in the best local botanical facial cleansers? Who is kindest and most generous, hosting big organic-food potlucks and sharing lovers? Polyamory got partners like me into public-facing love-triangle tangles on the regular: no matter how much I jogged, danced, or ate clean, attempting to rid myself of the little tummy "meat pouch" Aiden teased me about, I dreaded these social displays of wellness, which could lead him easily, I felt, to the impulse to "love" whoever looked most well. My jealousy, I thought, was merely a flaw in myself, my uncommunal attitude, because toxic positivity decrees that if you can't "manifest" what you want in life, *you're* doing something wrong.

There was also apathy in the festi-circuit: people called each other "hon," or "love," or "beautiful" to avoid having to recall each other's individual names. Altruism, always championed, failed often to translate to actions like voting, volunteering, or donating. While traditions from indigenous or ancient Eastern communities were venerated, it was easier to imitate them—borrow bindis and moccasins for festivals—than to aid in material improvement of their lives and social positions.

And there was hypocrisy: bodies made pure by clean eating during the day were wracked by party drugs at night. Mothers, celebrated socially as the spiritual mirrors of nature, were often left unsupported, undereducated, and underemployed without healthcare once freewheeling romantic partners left them single in the impending face of fatherhood.

One year, a year of many forest fires in the mountains, a mini music festival was held, and drug-laced dancers could be seen spinning and pounding the dirt to deep bass while, behind them, smoke billowed.

Trees and creatures burned.

Yet because I loved Aiden, and because I was intrigued by an alternate vision of a future, I wasn't quite ready, yet, to give up this scene.

"Live in the moment" was the mantra.

"The present is your greatest present."

So I stuck around longer, just to see.

I was a little worried, for a chunk of some months, that Aiden was still in love with his ex, Lindsay. She'd dumped him after he'd gotten up to some funny business with another girl at an out-of-town party, and I knew he regretted his mistake. It had been a year or so since they'd split, but he still spoke of her.

I regarded her with some suspicion.

Short, pale, unsmiling, with somehow three front teeth and enviably thick eyebrows, she was a strange, dramatic kind of beauty. She worked at the local bar where our friends went for happy hour, where the whole town, it seemed, went dancing on weekends, where she unsmiled at customers and sold them snacks. A few times, she bagged up our cookies or chips or beer to go, and never warmly.

When I asked him about her demeanor, Aiden laughed. "She's just weird."

But her presence, in addition to being intense, was alert: I sensed she knew who I was. We had a few awkward interactions. And I could see why he'd loved her: though enigmatic and quiet, she was obviously quite smart. When I ran into her in group conversations among our mutual friends, I listened to her explain, intelligently and economically, her perceptions about a range of subjects, like local politics and business, nearby canyon river ecology, the social history of Arizona. I wished we hadn't met the way we had. I would have liked, I thought, to be numbered among her many loyal friends. We had, irritatingly, the same passion for the arts: Lindsay, a painter and art history major who'd logged study time in Europe, and I, an eager baby writer who'd just, along with the owners' son Sal, decided we needed an online listing service in addition to our hostel time-share exchange, so other hostels and traveling creatives could find and match up with each other.

One day I heard Lindsay had applied to work at the hostel. Surprised, I wrote her a note: a gentle reminder that I worked there, and that I also lived onsite, in case it would make her uncomfortable for us to work and live so closely. She wrote me back that that was fine, she was sorry about the awkwardness we'd had, that she'd like to get to know me better.

I must admit I was charmed.

"Maybe she's not so bad," I said to Aiden.

He laughed. "Of course not!"

Thereafter, on morning shifts, I spied her moving from room to room with the other cleaners, carrying her tub of supplies to scrub sinks and swab toilets. Was she smiling a little at guests as she wiped up the toast crumbs from the communal breakfast table? Sometimes she'd smile at me, I thought: closed lips but the corners of her mouth turned up.

Then one day she came to the front desk where I checked guests in and out.

"I want to help you with that arts project you're doing."

She meant the little arts resource exchange website I'd been scheming. Our mutual friends must have mentioned it.

"It sounds really useful."

I was shocked.

"Do you want to meet after work and talk?" she asked.

My shift didn't end till midnight, I told her.

"Sure," she said, and my eyes must have been the size of saucers.

But sure enough, she came back. We sat in the low-lit after-hours lobby to talk: what could and would we do next to help creative workers connect? She was matter-of-fact, ready to go. I didn't have to ask how much time she wanted to commit—she was *in*. After our second meeting, she began to refer to the business as "our" project. And little by little, over the ensuing months, I started to spend as much time with her as I did with Aiden, fundraising. Designing a website. Running user test groups. Researching how a website scales. She drove us through the desert, once, to a nearby town to pitch at a statewide grant forum.

Eventually we added her name to the paperwork. Paid together for more website work, then hired an affordable developer, taking out some loans to do it.

My colleague boundary with Lindsay began to dissolve, and when I went to discuss our next steps with our business, she and I talked, finally, about our experiences dating Aiden: how we loved his good qualities but struggled with some things. We began to talk, over time, about our families too, our pasts and dreams.

When she told me she didn't smile broadly because she was embarrassed about her teeth, I felt a deep pang in my chest for her. She was, of course, just as vulnerable as anybody.

We rebuilt our art exchange site, added a journal component. We grew.

5

One weekend, Aidan and I drove with a group of festi-kids across the desert to Coachella, the mega music festival in sunburnt Southern California. Down the mountains and out into the Mojave, past energy windmills we went. The driver was rolling on ecstasy. He passed people fast on an eventually two-lane highway, which didn't seem to bother anyone in the car but me. After we stopped for drinks at a little dusty highway bar, my hands, however, unclamped a little, and I piled more happily back into the cramped backseat.

I didn't know anyone at the campsite when we arrived, a mega-grouping of tents past hundreds of doppelganger rows of other cars and tents, but after more booze and some cornhole games and frisbee golf, I forged a casual chumminess.

Aiden painted necklaces on my collarbones.

We drank and danced at the campground all night, then after breakfast the following day we walked together in groups toward the stages slung with snacks, canteens, and little hip packs of pills into the strengthening sun. One or two people held tall homemade poles topped with animal-themed flags: the way for lost camp-friends to find their group in the crowds. I could see all eight stages from the hill, before campground dropped into carnival and the bass began to shimmer through my body. The final division was the checkpoint, where purses and backpacks were searched, waistbands and ankles patted.

"Here, take this. They won't check *you*," Aiden said, pressing a clear plastic baggie into my palm. Apparently, despite my attempts to shed my obvious nerdiness, ordering online my bright tights and tie-dyed top, and even one chain-linked ring-bracelet combo disappointingly referred to as a "slave bracelet," I didn't pass as a real festi maven. I noticed, though, that the rent-a-cops at security were checking *everyone*'s purse. I also didn't really have time to argue with Aiden in the swell of bodies moving us forward. So I snuck the little baggie into my hat, which remained on my head during the search.

On the other side of the checkpoint, I opened the baggie and poured out a little pair of tiny white discs. When I put one on my tongue, colors brightened, the air around me lightened, and breathing seemed easier.

I watched the others dose themselves too, taking plentiful slugs of water from canteens.

Then we all went together in search of oblivion:

SBTRKT's wobbly resonance.

Interpol's moody climb to climax.

The frank and clompy sauciness of Scissor Sisters.

The ethereal Erykah Badu.

My memories of hearing these artists at previous times in my life meshed and retraced themselves as time slowed and deepened: Quirky Animal Collective, alone in my room. Broken Social Scene's tinkling reverie, on a first date with a man I'd met at a bus stop. The Twelves' disco-dub dissolution of Radiohead's "Reckoner" in the car, on the highway here, packed into a cramped backseat before the beer and the beat finally eased me into surrender.

All my memories gathered and merged.

I slipped inside myself, unnoticed, and observed.

Eventually the day disappeared, and when the bass swelled at nightfall and the crowds got chaotic, I seemed to return. The headliner, Arcade Fire, arrived on the main stage, and we swam our way through the sea of other partygoers to see them play. The piano roared. The band was so far away we had to watch them on a screen, while the crowd of maybe a hundred thousand, surging below and around us, caused us to sway when it swayed. We faced the same direction together to listen, as the band re-created for us all the sensations we'd each had when we first heard them.

And yet, returning to camp in the buzz and glow afterward, the lines for bathrooms and dusty showers stretched too long again. The constant thud of stereo-bass began to drone. Snatches of conversations sounded circular now. And I grew restless for the weekend to end, to return to a community connected with a more common contemporary reality. This fun was good fun, but it didn't, couldn't, extend beyond itself. In the face of other folks living and working all around this camp, scrimping and saving for basic needs, our $350+ weekend seeded unease. And most of the people here, I'd noticed too, were white, which made me wonder whether people of color didn't have access, financial or social, and/or whether they had better things to do with their time.

So I could lie for just one more night, listening under the stars I knew were up there past the floodlights, and try to let in smaller voices: I could make out a cricket now and then, scraping its legs together in the grass near our tent, putting out a call for its own kind of company. Then the next day we'd all awaken and return to shared concerns: politics, money, morality, equity, along with a strange sudden suction of sound. The old orange groves of the Coachella Valley, flattened into unified field, would be littered with trash when we piled into the SUVs again, miles of misshapen new crops covering land that used to bloom with fruit.

When I got home again, the silence of my bedroom was deafening.

I told my friend Syd about it, sitting late together afterward.

The music was great, I admitted: "mostly." We'd had some moments of blissful erasure.

But then I told her of the rest of it. Syd was a single mom, mostly working class, and she lived mostly outside the excesses of that scene. She was also a newly minted lobbyist, often for local tribal concerns, and had opinions about festi-culture's culturally appropriative habits.

"It's so hypocritical," she agreed, as I explained the field of trash we'd driven away from. "Some environmentalism!"

We drank our cab sauv and scoffed. Between tipsy-brave bar patrons approaching to try to speak with Syd, we vented. Syd was beautiful: shocking opalescent eyes, dimpled milky skin, soft curves, and even softer auburn hair far longer than mine would grow. As the longer-nosed and less lovely lady, I had become practiced at telling lecherous barside intruders, seeking to speak to Syd, to fuck off. Over time and repetition, my manners had faded. I didn't smile like Syd did. I didn't giggle, which she did when she was nervous. I wasn't hired for a lobbying job out of a bartending job, without a degree, by a lawyer I'd first refused to date, like Syd was. But although her beauty, her magnetism maybe, in some ways afforded her privileges outside the realm of most people's experience, Syd was deep. Past the giggles and sinfully good skin, Syd was smart. She hadn't quite finished college, but she read. She leaned, politically, into anarchy, and didn't demur from explaining, to surprised potential dissuaders, exactly why. On days she had her daughter, we'd brunch and philosophize about the nature of freedom. On nights she didn't, we browsed local art, went dancing. Sometimes we took road trips. We bemoaned our weird love lives, shared our yearnings to move to warmer places someday, to travel, support creativity, and she even told me she could help host visiting artists in one of her spare rooms.

One day, while sitting with Syd, I got a phone call. It seemed that Aiden, who'd gone to another SoCal music festival, this one a cross between commercialized Coachella and artsier Burning Man, had been arrested. Apparently he'd given a joint to someone who'd asked him for weed, then the man threw a ten-dollar bill in his lap and cuffed him for intending to "sell."

Syd immediately offered to drive me (I didn't have a car) to go and try to get him out of jail. We drove all day across the desert, slept in a Walmart parking lot, and pulled into San Bernardino early the following morning, where we found the jail, large and looming.

A silver monolith against a backdrop of fresh-paved blacktop and field grass, it made my palms start to sweat as we approached it. I'd hobbled out, ten years before, from a military building not unlike this one—enormous and secured—securing two broken ribs with my hand and sanity with the thinnest thread of hope. Syd was one of the only people in town who knew about that time: that once, when young, I'd signed up as an army reservist, on call to kill to pay for college. I'd never had a stronger aversion than to what I witnessed there.

"Let me talk to them," Syd said, sensing my agitation. "I have some background."

Sure enough, as I listened to her speak with the Plexiglased entry guard, court-system jargon in hand, terminologies I did not know, I knew she would get what we needed: information.

It came out that they were overfilled: there'd been an abundance of arrests at the festival, with only a certain number of hours left to process and charge people. Aiden had been there too long now without being charged, so he could leave.

We waited for him, spent a day on the beach all together, then went home. Driving through the night back to Arizona, I wondered, while Syd and Aiden slept, if Aiden's brush with incarceration would divert his sense of defiance. Would he get a normal job? Get in line and get legal? But Aiden was angrier than ever at "the man" and delved even deeper into ways of operating around the normal: more spiritual diets, meditation, more alternative community. He still stole groceries, sold psychedelics, skipped out on student loans.

At an upcoming little local festival, which had made a concerted effort to improve upon the big festival model, Aiden would get to play some of the songs he'd made. The tickets were more affordable than Coachella—just enough to pay performers—and attendees could also volunteer to earn tickets if they couldn't buy them. Everyone who bought or worked for a ticket signed a contract to clean up their trash and "leave no trace" that they'd danced and camped there, and one of the volunteer jobs was to scour the festival grounds for trash after everyone else had left.

After Coachella, I had some reservations about the insularity of festivals in general, but I liked the festival's main leaders, a young husband-and-wife team who treated the long weekend more like a laboratory from which useful learning and stress relief could be carried back to reality. They made an effort to book not only commercially popular acts but also Navajo hoop dancers, obscure regional bluegrass bands, a Colombian circus troop, and a variety of local painters. They wanted to host a good swath of workshops: hour-long mini-classes on such topics as poetry, methods for countering substance abuse, pesticide-free gardening, and divine ratios in nature. Since I'd failed to become a proficient DJ but still wanted to participate in township hobbies with my partner, I turned to a more humdrum and practical means of involvement: making the workshop schedule.

Spreadsheets. E-mails. Calendars.

I had a hard time choosing seminar leaders: there were more applicants wanting to trade workshop labor for tickets than there were available time slots to offer. Who would have a voice, get to teach and speak their ideas? Who got a public platform? I stretched the schedule long, adding extra offerings to each morning and evening to accommodate more, and still had to turn prospective teachers away. I scrounged up decor, used carpeting, and pillow seating for the workshop space. When the weekend of the festival arrived, I made sure seminar leaders got their attendance passes and their mic and projection equipment, and that attendees had materials they needed too: pens and paper, water, directions to the Porta-Potties.

Meanwhile, I watched Aiden run cables, hunting for plugs and power cords to extend and connect electricity to amps, speakers, and subs.

"What exactly *is* an amplifier?" I asked one day on a snack break, and he explained: Simply put, an amp takes a small electrical signal and grows it. Amplifiers push sound pulses into more transmissive fabrics: electrical and metal materials, then air. Most DJs don't use amps: they plug directly into subwoofer speakers. Amps are mostly for live-instrument musicians, whose notes, not prerecorded together, have several more channels of material to bridge to make their sound loud.

How much harder, I thought, to get an original new sound to squeak out than one premanufactured by a machine. And perhaps also, how hard to resist some sampling to shortcut? But was it also as easy as it looked to borrow other people's music and stitch it together with other stuff into some kind of meaningful smoothness?

I was curious enough to scrounge up some credit card space, buy a controller, and download hours of music: sexy deep house, electro-swing, and eighties. I began to twist knobs, press buttons. I wanted to understand how to move not only myself but a roomful of people together: make unity. But it's easier said than done to create the circumstances through which unity can begin to be.

Even when I successfully snipped and restitched electronic notes, and learned how to find files that didn't shed data when sound was compressed into them and didn't render it weak and fuzzy when amplified, and even though I practiced for hours blending rhythms, tinkering tempos, bumping BPMs up or down to match and merge and sync the end of one song to the start of another, it was very hit or miss. I consulted local veteran DJ Emtron about what I was hit-or-missing.

Emtron reminded me that listening is just as much a part of performing as anything: you can't make choices without feedback. You stitch the past to the present and then plan what's next. What kind of music has just been played? Are people energized for motion, ready to meet a nice big heartrending wall of sound? Do they need a respite from hard-driving refrains?

You can't separate a context surrounding you from your decisions. When, sometimes, you're in the middle of a song and the mood shifts and you need to make a sudden change, Emtron said, "Just stopping and starting a new song is underrated."

Cue it up. Put your finger on the trigger button, then cross your other fingers and press down.

The weekend of the local festival, I set up camp with Aiden, though he barely rested in the tent. Both of us were busy with tasks, but it had grown later than late. As I lay alone into the wee hours of night, muffled festival noises swirling into my sleep, I admitted to myself I really probably should leave my lover.

Being with Aiden hurt on an almost monthly basis, sometimes even weekly, and I was learning that you can't fake unity. I tried to accept about Aiden what he claimed he could not change: his need to explore sexual intimacy with *women*, plural. And for a while, I almost could get on board. I sort of could. I tried, and he tried to meet me partway, with arbitrary rules about who could do what and when so as not offend the other (I even tried to dabble with other men), though none of it satisfied us both. He wanted freedom, and I wanted ease: no secret surrenders in the dark, no slips into subterfuge, no running into stories about baby-faced Sami or redheaded Roxanne, evidence of sex sandwiched into people's silence at cafes, or guilty love notes tucked into pockets.

But by then our memories were stacking up too: our lighthearted walks around town, leisurely soup making, soothing back rubs. Every time I thought of leaving, I thought of us, chasing down joy together in the powerful center of a dance floor, or in one of the nearby mountain meadows, and it became too hard to go.

One deep winter night, in the aftermath of another romantic rumor about him that I deeply suspected to be true, I wandered Flagstaff alone, late and lost. My spirit was rent, and in mirroring it, I'd knifed up a painting I'd made for Aiden, of a lovely bright swirl of colors twisting together into a bird, the animal I love best: that creature that speaks to me most of freedom. Now there was no bird in the painting, as there were no birds in the trees: it was snowy, and I felt caged by my loyalty to this love. I was also becoming someone I didn't like. I'm not the crazy B-word who knifes up artwork. At least I didn't want to be.

I didn't know what else to do, so I put on my boots and crunched through the snow uphill toward the hospital. I walked for an hour or so, got above the town and looked down over it, glimmering, low-lit. Then I still didn't know what else to do, so I walked back down.

"Hey, Lydi," a voice said then, softly, midway down San Francisco Street. "How ya doing?"

Only three people call me Lydi: Uncle Steve, roommate Rachel, and B-boy Sonni. There stood Sonni in the street. I told him how I was.

"Oh, girl," he said. "Come with me."

He didn't say where. We traced along through ice-encrusted streets to the dance studio he time-shared with other dancers and teachers. Sonni could use it after hours with his key, and we entered, away from the cold.

"Let's dance," he said. He led me onto the pretty pinewood floor. I replied that I didn't feel like dancing, and that I didn't even know how to do it without a crowd around, a larger entity to disappear into.

"Just follow me," he said.

One movement he made, with one foot or arm, then another, with another, for me to imitate.

Sonni, in addition to being a breathtaking B-boy, wresting pop locks and low spins from his constantly training body, was also a hip-hop experimental dancer, artist producer, and choreographer, and won regional powwows as a grass dancer. His range of motion far exceeded mine, but in pushing myself to new shapes—a sweep here, a step or bend or twirl there—my mind shifted away from its love-loss-loop panic.

So for an hour or so, I just followed.

It created rotation, reprogramming.

My mind began to move forward, and I didn't need music, or a sea of bodies surrounding me, to remember. I remembered, in the quiet, how flower petals curve to hold dew. How bodies on a dance floor move like ghosts.

6

Syd, savior of Aiden from jail and of my sanity so often, was my best dining date. She was the one who told me how to eat properly when I was told to cut wheat from my diet, because she too had gluten issues, so no soy sauce, and be careful around soups and sauces for the sneaky flour thickeners.

We decided, one day after work, to get sushi. We were chopsticking seaweed salad into our mouths (no miso: it might have hidden wheat) at our favorite spot on the main downtown drag when we saw a somewhat paltry string of skeleton-people, or rather skeleton-dressed mostly middle-aged white people, most with young kids in tow, tailed by a local Brazilian-style drumming group, make a snail-paced journey past our window.

Syd cracked wise about cultural appropriation: the Day of the Dead wasn't a costume party for white people.

Chewing, ever conflict-averse, I conciliated. "Well, at least they're trying to get their kids interested in other cultures. Right? Mimicry is flattery?"

They weren't, at least to my mind, in the same category of offender as my recent French hostel guests who'd dressed up like Western movie "Indians" and gone downtown to get drunk, fake stomp-dancing in faux headdresses. The yuppies today seemed attempting reverence for, rather than mocking, Mexicans.

Syd disagreed: even *if* it was well intentioned, the behavior was colonial. Theft, by imitation, of ritual and art was as harmful as stealing land. And how much easier, she asked, it is to pat yourself on the back for wearing a Kokopelli T-shirt or trying yoga once than to really invest in people living on the margins? Instead of imitating, let's listen, volunteer, donate, protest, vote.

While I could see this perfectly fair point, I will admit that I did not understand, then, Syd's vehemence. I wondered if there weren't bigger fish to fry: like white nationalists, who want non-whites (along with non-Christians, queer folks, and feminists) dead or enslaved, and who make up or adapt old mythologies to further cement their hate into common culture.

But this was important too, Syd insisted: cultural appropriation caused insidious harm, whether I could understand how deeply or not. You have to listen, she said, when people tell you things hurt them. Example: when someone doesn't think they're sexually harassing you, but you tell them so, they should hear you and change their behavior until they "get it" (even if they never do).

Which I could see. People do make excuses not to change: we're complacent. Marginalized people don't have time to wait for privileged people to *decide* to be sensitive to their needs.

I agreed with this, and yet it seemed important, too, that changes be encouraged to occur internally, not simply as socially pressured veneer: that people be offered information and given some space to integrate the complexity of equity, not just be jammed into formal social shifts, or shoehorned into more subtle ones, which they didn't understand and might always resent. A person can say the right things in public, after all, and still be secretly racist.

In which case, behavioral policing would need to be constant.

Legislatures would be at risk of backsliding, always, into hierarchy, whenever people without equity as a priority came to power. For the first time in my grown-ass life, I felt like a proponent of "conversion."

"We should spread the word!" I said.

But Syd said education failed, or at least it wasn't enough: too slow. And in lieu of expeditious understanding, shame was fair game.

But where do all the shamed people go, I asked, once pushed apart from progressives for not being progressive enough fast enough? They don't simply cease to exist, they just risk being embraced and absorbed by worse. Shamers aren't that good at letting canceled people back into the fold, even after apologies and penances have been performed.

Then you have a swelling small army who lump all calls for change together as inhibitors of "liberty."

"Well, violence works," Syd said.

I'm pretty sure my eyes bugged.

When I found some words, I mumbled something about how violence was the same shitty method of social change that historical aggressors have always used, the method we're trying to move away from.

"But we're not," Syd said.

"Right. If physical force really does work for change, then why do we *still* have to use it? It's not a stand-in for justice," I said. "E*veryone* thinks their own acts of violence are righteous."

As I spoke and gestured, I could feel myself float into memory: me, in a field with other soldiers, stuffing bayonets into stuffed straw dummies. In foxholes, aiming at dark paper silhouettes, all features obscured by the need to win, the will to power. The right way to do things. The end attempting to justify the means.

Oxygen rushed, unbeckoned, into my body. My cheeks flamed red and my stomach twisted small. I could feel my muscles contracting automatically. Even in trying to defend peace, I was returning to a readiness for war.

Returning to it is too easy, too tempting, a sickly sweet shortcut that rarely reaches the intended destination.

Like a train run away, as we went back and forth, our argument grew by dimensions: the history of American racism and withholding of rights, the roles marginalized peoples and socially privileged people ought to play in changemaking, tactics that were permissible and effective to correct social wrongs. Syd wanted to balance the playing field of American social sins fast. I doubted her methods: the idea that any certain people should be allowed or disallowed certain behaviors by bloodline or birthright.

Violence aside, did preachy Facebook posts or street protests matter that much to men and women in real power—who weren't her friends on Facebook, and who didn't care if underprivileged people took time off from work to wear their feet out on the concrete with clever picket signs?

I still retained a hopefulness that, if given more information about how history, religion, psychology, sociology, and policy all impact equity, people could start to seek social justice on their own while understanding it must be built together.

Either way, I told myself, at least we weren't just another two women arguing over men. And as we argued, I remember thinking about how we'd eventually agree, if even just to disagree, or talk more about these issues over time. We would go back to being Syd and Lyd, meeting in the middle. We'd do some research and return to discuss. Syd would rest her hand on my collarbones and tell me again: "I love you." Our friendship, with its steady concern for the needs, values, and time of the other, would overcome our opinions about the culture wars, and we'd return to co-scheming the future into perfection and poking fun at bar-stool pricks.

Yet, several hours into this conversation, we were sliding in separate directions.

Between the sushi bar, another attempted dinner date, and then several social media squabbles over the span of several ensuing weeks, I cherry-picked some Gandhi quotes, Syd said my perspectives were naïve, I said her willingness to move toward violence was irresponsible, and we stopped speaking.

I dreamt of her often afterward, thought about her constantly, argued with her in my mirror while brushing my teeth, as I moved across the country again and again over the ensuing years.

"Your privilege is showing," I mumbled at her while I scrubbed: Syd who'd been hired, in part, for her beauty, and who knows how many people agreed with her politics just to see her smile?

"What kind of anarchist shops at Anthropologie?" And so forth.

I told myself Syd talked a tough game and wore badass boots but she herself never really picketed, at least not that I'd seen. Nor had she seen violence up close: felt how *hard* it was to stop physical struggle once it started, felt it trap you.

And yet . . .

Fast forward some seven years. I still didn't think shame would save us, but with a federal administration moving toward fascism, and my move to a more (overtly) racially fraught city, I began to ask:

Had I been naïve?

Had it been willful?

At least the riots are honest, I thought, as I went to BLM marches and watched white participants take selfies, masked up, so helpful. Watched the well-connected lawyer couple wield weapons from their patio one year at peaceful protestors, with few meaningful repercussions, while black people were and are brutally overpoliced. Confederate flags flap all too frequently from the backs of trashy pickups, not to mention the near-constant pushback against reparations, which seem warranted.

Was I, I asked myself, just like the festi-kids Syd and I used to mock back in Flag, who claimed to "care about everyone" but still just put their own pleasures first, like all the mainstreamers they spurned? Was I dancing at the party while proverbial mountains burned behind me?

Conversely, I don't want to step into autopilot, allowing my anger to own me.

There's discipline in pushing for progress, developing neither complacency nor an ugly, all-too-common addiction to ire.

How do we, the people, meet all needs equally, not just the needs of a historically favored handful? And how do we do it now?

Maybe it begins with some humility. Lost in liminality, I tend to listen more. My thinking's incomplete. My attempts to improve end sometimes in error.

How to be good? How to help?

Maybe I can learn something from my foray into festival life after all: I'm the amp and not the instrument here, and I should seek other speakers to support. Then ask them how.

7

One day in Flag, about a month after Aiden moved into my house, and two weeks after he decided he suddenly "wasn't in love anymore," I walked to a downtown patio. I'd decided enough was enough: no more sorrow. I was ready to let go of the vision that we could work, because I needed a vision of myself with dignity.

I'd been to AA meetings with my dad at as young as age twelve, and though I'd learned some things I likely didn't need to know—like how if you get drunk and dry-swallow pain pills for your impending hangover, then fall asleep, they can burn a hole through your throat because you didn't wash it down and then you'll die—or maybe I do need that info?—there was one very good piece of data I saved, this adage: that the definition of insanity is doing the same thing over and over and expecting different results.

"Change the song," I coached myself per Emtron's performance advice. "Stop, line up the new song, then push the trigger button."

It was a beautiful day. The patio was full of friends. My life wasn't so bad. And on this patio this day, I met Tim.

Funny.

Big smile.

Bright eyes.

I liked it that he cracked himself up with his own jokes, which were smart, that he had a lot of male friends, and also that his perspective of reality included the not-so-rosy aspects all the festi-kids tried to dismiss: that you might need to have a real job instead of living on the same food stamps you complain about, that you can't merely meditate all the world's problems away, that sometimes people really can suck, though some of them try not to. I found it refreshing that he was an atheist and yet maintained a dedicated moral system. He played music on real live instruments, wrote angsty, wild, and tender songs. I also found it refreshing thta he could pin down aggressive assholes when they got too drunk at his bar: try not to hurt them, but kick them the fuck out. He tried not to call the cops. He listened when people talked. I could see how hard he tried to find common ground with people, even those he knew he disagreed with.

I asked him out, and pretty quickly, after two open mics and some late-night walks, we felt like teammates, of the tender type:

he liked holding hands in public. Said I was easy to love. We went together to events and hung out equally happily at home. After dating him for a month or two, I found myself crying one day: how much I had hurt myself by staying so long with Aiden. How mean to myself I had been.

Once, I showed Tim how to get two songs to kiss one another in a computer, and though a purist instrumental musician, he said, grudgingly, "Okay, this is harder than it looks." He was delighted when he succeeded, his glee at the sonic combination obvious and contagious.

We both liked learning, and we both yearned for unity, with similar boundaries around it.

He helped me carry my groceries, and he never stole his own.

He even carried Faith down the hostel stairs when she called during dinner to ask for a ride to the hospital.

Faith, my friend and hostel colleague from England, had bad food allergies which seemed to be progressing into epilepsy and other things.

At the same open mic where I first spent time with Tim, Faith had come in with her guitar, and while she waited to play, suddenly her face had paled and she leaned into a table.

"Does your food have peanuts in it?" she'd asked, motioning to my open to-go box.

"No . . . ?" I'd said, mid-bite, suddenly confused by my noodles.

"Seafood?"

My smile faded, as I came to understand I'd somehow made her sick. She had to sit down outside, and then go home. I couldn't even bring her water because she said tap water had chlorine, which could hurt her. She didn't brush her teeth, as toothpaste contained additives, ate no meat, drank no booze (she said she had no liver function left), only bought raw organic produce and bottled purified water. She kept a water filter to screw onto showerheads for bathing.

She'd told me about her home, a farming community north of Manchester: lots of wheat and DDT. Her immune disorders started young: she'd shown me photos of herself, skeletal, lying on a couch at age eighteen, dropped out of school at Cambridge and ready to die. She'd almost given up hope and was so weak they took her to the hospital. While the rest of her was paralyzed, she used one arm and hand to scroll the internet for answers, eating just one grape at a time, until she found information on autoimmune and dietary disease. Then, even though her English doctors dismissed her suggestion that her mysterious illness might be improved by better food, she stopped eating their sandwiches, their puddings, everything processed, requesting only produce, and that's, she said, when she got better.

For a while she seemed fine in Flagstaff too, beaming with her newfound freckles, smacking her legs happily and joking of loving her "big fat thighs," because she could walk again, even out on trails in the peaks, through stands of chittering aspen. Her hair had grown long in soft curls, her cheeks were rosy, she laughed often, and she'd made good friends, she said, people who were kind and also believed in the power of food: of molecules, of chemistry, of energy. When the evening hostel crowd brought their dinners to the couches to chat with other guests, Faith declined their refreshments, but she'd regale them with semi-funny tales from her odd, adventurous life: how she lived in a tent between her time in the hospital and coming here, how she kept away from her family and walked miles into town for free WiFi, worked online as a health counselor, mail-ordered a certain brand of pesticide-free dates to her tiny plot of land. People were charmed by her strength, her wry humor, her optimism.

And when we hung out, I felt humbled by her humility.

"I don't mind scrubbing toilets!" she said. "It's quite satisfying!"

"You're so British!" I laughed. "How orderly!"

"Work keeps my mind off of things."

We'd go shopping: venture off into the aisles at the health food store, where I piled cans of beans and boxed gluten-free pastas alongside her produce.

While I picked out my various wine varietals, Faith stacked water that had been purified.

And when I expressed sympathy about her limitations, she said, "I'm just happy to be alive."

Yet she declined. Once, I watched her fall in the parking lot, and our coworker took to her to the hospital. Pretty soon the falls became frequent and seizures started. Faith could sense their onset and would go to hide in the bathroom to shake and flap out of view of hostel guests, up to, she told me, twenty times a day. As her hospital bills stacked up, many brains began brainstorming for answers. There were experts in Phoenix, recommended one of Faith's roommates. Maybe, I thought, the Mayo Clinic had a study she could try. Faith was afraid to begin conventional therapies for epilepsy because she'd been allergic to certain medicines before and had an anaphylactic reaction. So meantime she tried to control her condition the way she always had: with diet.

"Tomatoes can be triggers," she told me: something about seizures and electricity in the body and the food.

"Sugar makes it worse." So fruit was out for now.

Amidst this, Faith's tourist visa was expiring, so she'd have to go home for a while and apply for a student visa to return for longer. I took her to the storage unit she'd rented, which would store her things while she was back in England. A friend had given me his old truck when he left the country, and we chugged over to the less stylish, more pragmatic part of town, the part that still looked more like a lumberjack locale than a tourist destination. There we punched in the gate code to a steel-gray-and-orange complex, found her unit—a small cube, maybe four or six feet square, stacked atop another—and tossed our stuff in.

"How did I accumulate so many things?" she asked. I nodded appreciatively. It was a lot, mostly cookware purchased new to keep her meals from cross-contamination by our secondhand and well-used hostel implements. Also bags of dresses and boots from the hippie shops downtown. And all her books. Her dormmates, I thought, would be gleeful for more space.

After it all went in, there was still a bit of room for us to sit and dangle our legs over the equally small unit below.

"This is all I want," Faith said, a fast-setting sun causing her eyes to crinkle, "just a little space to call my own, where no one can bother me. Maybe I'll come and hang out here when I get back."

Then she turned to me.

"I'm going to miss you," she said.

"I'm going to miss you too, Faith," I said, and I meant it, and we hugged.

But what I didn't also say was that I was also quietly relieved to have a break from her troubles on a day-to-day basis. Her new meds, after she eventually caved and began to take them, seemed to have sent her on a roller-coaster. Some days, she was high and happy—shopping, falling in love with a new boyfriend, getting her nose pierced, riding on the back of a motorcycle. Other days, everything seemed to be wrong, Faith's body and soul twisted together in sickness. As guilty as I felt about it, I looked forward to more space for myself, to not feeling so absorbed.

8

One day during this era, my brother came to visit. He flew into Phoenix, and I met him at the Flagstaff train station shuttle stop. Where we strolled downtown, the mountains in the distance framed the buildings into tableau. The sun was close and bright, the air was clear, and we'd run into four different people I knew within five blocks.

"Geez, how do you live here?" Bobey asked. "You can't walk ten steps without someone stopping you to talk."

"Is that a bad thing??" I asked, it never having occurred to me that it would be.

"And besides—" I spread my arms out toward the peaks "—isn't it beautiful?"

"Well, yeah," he said. "It's nice, but I would never get anything done."

Bobey lived in New York now, where things are efficient. In New York he worked in tech, and went by his proper birth name, not the childhood nickname I used.

We waved back to a little group waving to us from across the street.

"Like, I bet everyone knows everyone else's beeswax."

When he said it, I realized it. Everyone sure knew Tim and I were hitting a rough patch. Apparently, when you've been cheated on a bunch by a previous partner, everything looks like flirtation. And like many folks in town, we bar-gued.

"It's a pretty interdependent place," I acknowledged.

I told him how the town functions as a unit, the boundaries between people partially eroded by time and proximity. If the mood of the town is bleak—say, construction commences on yet another student housing mega-complex, a stranger is found smeared on the train tracks, or another younger-than-average party liver fails—the whole town mourns as one.

One of the things Bobey wanted to do while visiting was to help Lindsay and me on our burgeoning arts website. We filmed a video to promote it to a business growth program up in the old historic hotel where Lindsay was manager now. When we finished, we had cocktails and finger food down in the lobby, and Bobey met Tim. Then Daniel popped over with Jonny Escalante.

I told Bobe about Faith, recently departed for England, since that whole situation was on all our minds.

"That's crazy!" he said of her story. "She lived in a tent?"

"I feel lucky when I talk to her," I admitted, "like everything I have to complain about is trivial."

I confided in Bobey, then, about:

My hefty student loan debt.

My lack of long-term job mobility.

A future still shaped like a question mark.

"Well," he said, "you're more risk-tolerant than me. My lease is up in four months. Then I might leave New York. Wanna come visit for a while?"

He told me everything was walkable or easily accessible by train: jobs, museums, universities, another kind of nightlife, other artistic communities.

"You could see how it compares to this."

I thought about it after he left: the offer of a lifetime, really. If you're any kind of an ambitious or curious young American, you don't turn down a chance to live in the West Village for four months, rent free. I began to tell folks, gently, that I was taking a hiatus. Hostel owner Lina said I could have my job back if/when I returned. My friends weren't going anywhere. Tim and I had a few ugly fights and broke up, or sort of broke up, or took a break for the moment.

So I booked my flight, packed my stuff, and flew through the morning to land at LaGuardia. My brother picked me up at the subway, and when we emerged in his neighborhood, we discovered that a friend of mine from Flagstaff, Chris, worked right down the street from his walk-up. Chris, a writer, had bartended at the same wine bar I had, and she'd taught at the same university too. Already, in synchronous chaos, I felt right at home.

"We can put your bed here," Bobe said, holding out his arms to indicate the space between the fridge and the sink: a one-bedroom, allegedly, but there was no wall, so we would hang a curtain between my space and his.

"I'm your Kitchen Sister," I joked.

From Bobe's second-story apartment in the West Village, I gazed at a swath of red brick buildings, cross-cut by an intermittently bright sky. In the street below, grates above the subway blew up air that smelled as human (food, sweat, oil) as it felt wild, bursting forth suddenly when the train barelled through.

I was, by an odd streak of luck, able to work remotely, adjunct teaching.

Meantime, being a millennial, I had to try entrepreneurship. I got online, lined up a schedule: between temp-job appointments and job interviews, I set meetings, walked long concrete stretches of blocks to hear speakers and teachers of the trade. I tried to learn tech vocab—pitch deck, seed funding, angel investor—to demonstrate my industry savvy as I spoke with other website builders at these workshops, wielding words as a shield for my ignorance.

On weekends Bobe and I browsed the busy summer streets, meandered through museums and sat through tech seminars, relaxed into balmy early evening happy hours outside. I started to meet my brother's pals: artists all, it seemed, or entrepreneurs: interested, informed, full of energy and ideas. Most days, I felt naïve.

He went of town for work during the week, and then I was alone, a learner and observer in a crowd of eight million, unless Chris and I went for dinner, or to a reading. Inside the apartment, sound was muted. I was alone there too, grading my papers for students now across the country. The kitchen sink spurted water randomly, like a peeing ghost, when people in other units flushed their toilets. I read and wrote at length again with the windows wide open. Air swelled into the apartment, causing the curtains to float, then sucked them back out like a tide. After years of primarily bad festi-poems composed in a cramped tent, or hiding behind my hostel desk, my mind was working. And I was thinking.

"I feel like a kindergartener," I told Bobey as we passed yet another well-heeled young woman professional in movie-level makeup, a pricey coat, and a Gucci bag.

"Well, you look like one!" He laughed, poking at the hole in my T-shirt, pointing at my dingy tennies. I did wash my hair but hadn't styled it in years.

Maybe I *had* lived a little too long in my little town, I said to myself, got lazy. Not that I needed more makeup, or my brother's six-hundred-dollar dress shoes, but couldn't I knock it up a notch, try again to participate in the patterns of the larger world?

I could redirect, I realized, if I tried.

Far away from Flagstaff, the giant city machine moved and breathed beyond the fire escape. Outside, swimming through sidewalks of noise, my senses pulsed, time vanished, my feet ached, and jarring moments (people spitting, cursing, pushing, stridently ignoring each other) faded together, adhered to my sense of normality.

Then it was deeper autumn. The city air had cooled, and leaves were falling. A sense of slowing and of change was afoot, even as every crunching step onto the sidewalk was followed with an awareness of edges: things breaking off.

Halloween came, season of spirits.

Bobey and I smeared fake blood around our mouths, powdered our faces gray, and cabbed our freshly birthed zombie selves to a rooftop party on Times Square.

An old Portland pal from high school, Gavin, happened to be popping through town with his girlfriend, and they joined us.

On the rooftop, we caught up and carried forward, silhouettes of buildings stretching for miles against amber city light glimmer, extending past the heads of other costumed partygoers. Out there, identities artfully constructed, the engines of the city hummed bright in the night, begging more. Even there, on the unadorned concrete roof, more was beginning: huddles of otherworldly shadows, tendrilled and glinting, talking excitedly of travel, people, dreams.

They danced, lit cigars, imbibed. I stood still amidst the puffs of rising cigarette smoke, vented steam, grind music, still amidst the laughter swirling around me, and I knew I would not fit back into my former Flagstaff self.

Even if I returned, I realized, it couldn't be for long.

9

Tim called. Despite the fact that we were supposed to be apart, we talked most days, sharing the details of my time in the city and his life around town.

"Have you seen Faith lately?" I asked, but he hadn't. The time she was away from Flag, like mine, was mysterious. She'd alluded to unpleasant happenings in her life, the few times I'd reached her by e-mail, but gave no detail: working as a maid at a large country estate, then being let go; working in an Irish hostel and being, also, let go? When I asked, "How are you? How is your health?" she dodged the question and asked me instead. Eventually I got word that she'd returned to Flag, started school, but things hadn't gone that well.

One day, finally, she called. I was midway through toilet scrubbing in my brother's tiny bathroom when she told me her news, and at first I didn't notice the water trickling down my upheld arm from the toilet brush when I stopped, suddenly, to gaze westward out the window.

"What?" I thought I had misheard her.

Her tone calm, resigned, she repeated: she'd realized the hostel-cleaner boyfriend she was seeing had raped her.

Over the course of several conversations over several days, I tried to understand. Her boyfriend of several weeks (or months?) was a hippie kid, into auras and organics, who practiced capoeira and meditated visibly. I found him dumb and cocky, but was he also pushy?

I remembered a dirty mattress years back in Portland, and my seventeen-year-old sense of enclosure returning as Faith described the night it happened: it was the same night Tim had carried her sick body down the stairs and we'd driven together to the hospital.

She had never mentioned, in the car or at the hospital, that before we'd driven there something additionally bad had just happened. Her epilepsy, she said, and the meds, made her foggy. But now it returned: this memory of resting in a private room, post seizure, trying for some sleep and peace for the night. Her boyfriend had come by to see her, and they'd cuddled, but then he'd climbed on top. Faith, post seizure, was too weak to speak, and he either thought he had consent in her silence, or he didn't care if he didn't, even saying something like "This is so wrong."

I remembered as she spoke: another's willpower first softening, then suffocating, your own. You know you're about to be used. I was immediately sad.

I told her how sorry I was, told her to go tell Lina. Get that bad boyfriend kicked out! Had she called the police?

But when I spoke with her next—crickets for two weeks or so and then a call—she herself had been evicted. Her boyfriend had not. I was aghast. Why? She said Lina only cared about the business, and a rape would look bad. She was hedgy when I asked about police: she wouldn't want to risk her visa. Victims' advocates? They were no help.

I'd seen it before, and it always made me nervous: when a worker from the hostel really got the boot, they had roughly one day to pack and rehome, a difficult feat in a town with clogged, expensive rentals. Now Faith was at a motel.

Then she gave me more news: she had a miscarriage there, alone.

She read me a poem she wrote to the baby.

I didn't, then, know what to say. My ideas all sounded abstract. I wasn't there to see her, to hold her. I hated the sound of my distant advice, mentioning other potential services. When we hung up the phone, I felt useless.

And also confused. I trusted Lina. Word around work was that she'd even paid for some of Faith's med bills. Why would she boot *her* from the hostel and keep a potential predator around?

I kept calling my former coworkers, but only got whispers: The boyfriend was actually her ex-boyfriend, and that's why he said having sex again was "wrong." But he'd thought it was consensual.

Did Faith know they had broken up?

She'd been acting really weird, I was told, accusing people of stealing from her.

Was her memory misplacing things?

A week or two later, I learned she'd moved in with Annie, who'd broken up with Ricardo and left the hostel attic.

Osmosis—169

Then . . . nothing.

I called to ask for updates, but no one answered.

It went on for weeks, the vagueness. While I was pounding new pavement in the East, there was silence from the West.

Then Daniel, the engineering student, called me back and told me Faith apparently forgot she'd ever even dated her hostel boyfriend/rapist. What was first reported as a possible "rape by mistake" had turned, in her language now, into "violent, multiple" rapes, and she said another of our coworkers had masturbated in a dorm bed next to her, without her agreement.

After moving in with Annie, Faith claimed Ricardo repeatedly called and tried to coerce her into sex.

Her teachers at school stopped excusing her many absences.

She said she broke her back.

Then she thought she broke her ankle.

She claimed to have a brain tumor.

Then AIDS.

At this point Annie asked her to leave, our colleagues stopped engaging with her, and last anyone heard, she'd quit college. Someone saw her in a wheelchair with an oxygen tank, rolling slowly around Whole Foods for organics. Nobody knew what to think. How horrific, if all this was true. And how horrific if it wasn't. Which was worse?

When I got off the phone from this call, I sank into my brother's desk chair and looked listlessly through the little window. There was an early snow, and I watched its soft whiteness float down in blank paper pieces, covering the sidewalk.

When my brother came in, a little cap of white covering his head, he was stomping his feet and hugging a cup of to-go soup in his hands. He brushed off the snow, then stopped.

"What's up with you?"

I felt catatonic, but I said, "I'm confused."

Because I remembered: distrusting.

I remembered: dusting.

The Flagstaff hostel banister, then plant stands.

It had been snowing, the previous year.

Down the hall to the upstairs kitchen again: and there I'd found Faith, alone, cooking.

"Mmm," I said, "smells good!"

"Thanks!" she said, stirring. "Nothing special."

When I walked over to peer into the pot, the bright orange soup, steaming hot, surprised me.

And her voice, earlier that month, echoed back:

"Tomatoes can be triggers . . ."

I swear she'd blushed.

"How come you didn't say something?" Bobe asked.

I shrugged and held my hands high. Had I? I couldn't even recall.

Brain tumors. Broken bones. A miscarriage. Multiple rapes. A tower of terrors too many to count, stacked high with AIDS on top, now teetering. A Bad Friend of the Year award for me, who should have called Faith directly that day to try to clarify, but did not.

"Empathy deficit," an NPR interview with the National Empathy Museum mentioned, while I listened in from some other kitchen later. "Compassion fatigue."

Tonic immobility, Google says, is a term for paralysis that happens when an animal finds itself in duress: a possum or horned lizard plays dead in front of predators. Some female sharks will freeze during sex. Humans, too, can disassociate to protect: tonic immobility can set in during rape, or other trauma.

I, likewise, feel frozen, unable to move either toward or from Faith.

Could I have continued to help?

How much?

I argue with myself:

Could Faith really have been as statistically unlucky as she claimed? Could everything she told us have been true?

Or was her ravaged mind collapsing on itself, unable to distinguish fear from fact anymore?

Or did Faith have Munchausen's?

If so, was she lying to herself, or just to other people?

And how much? Were pieces of her story true, even if the whole of it crumpled?

Lauren Slater, in *Lying*, her memoir on that subject, writes that experts found epilepsy to be a common illness among Munchausen patients, and relates her own experiences of seizing at will, taking herself frequently to hospitals or allowing others to admit her repeatedly. She describes hungering for and relishing the sympathy of caretaking doctors, nurses, and nuns—all the kind affection that she never got at home.

She speaks about this as a kind of stealing: a theft of people's time.

Is that why so many people drifted away from Faith? A feeling that energy spent on her was, potentially, not really needed?

I realize, as I ponder Faith's failure to ever mention old friends, that maybe we Flagstaff folks were not the first friends to burn out on befriending her.

I still don't have any answers.

I still wonder if I'm wrong.

How much guilt will I carry with me, for how long, for stepping off this constant trauma train, only by abandoning my dear pal?

I'm also too confused, and too frightened, to find out.

I lost my faith in Faith that day, and I confess: I never called her again.

Even when she sent me one final text about some stuff I'd left in her storage unit, my fingers merely hovered above the keypad, lingering until I wrote nothing. I stared at my waiting phone screen until my inaction cemented itself into action: nonchoice my choice. I tucked her hanging question forever back into my pocket, and my own curling questions into circles. In lieu of knowing what else to do, I stacked up my need for freedom against Faith's need for help of one kind of another . . . then tiptoed quietly away.

10

Back in Flag, four months gone and working desk again, I stare into the void of our dark parking lot.

Tim's on his way home from a music tour, then we're doing something, for us, unconventionally conventional: getting hitched. Then we'll move to St. Louis for another bout of schooling, but for now a three-month pause to regroup. While we prepare to move onward, people's presence here persists. Former roommate Rachel will come to the wedding, as well as most of my hostel and many of his bartending coworkers. Our poet friends will read in lieu of scripture; musical compatriots will sing and DJ both. But there are some people we won't invite that I wish we could, had things turned out differently. I think a lot now of boundaries: who got to know, witness, and love what pieces of each other, and for how long.

How much damage we did to each other in the exchange.

It's now my last night of this work.

Luckily, it's slow; what guests are booked in have gone out onto the town. So I wait for the bedding to arrive in plastic bags, fill both washers, scoop the soap in, pour in the bleach, crank the dials far left, and close the lids. I wait for the stragglers to check in late. I wait for midnight.

I return to the kitchen, wash my hands, sit down on the couch with a magazine.

When it's still like this, I still feel at home. The lobby is ordered and quiet, but not silent: a wall clock ticks in the kitchen. The slow swoosh of tires and grumbling air brakes, muffled by our building's exterior brick, are still audible from long journeys down I-40. On occasion, I pick up scraps of chatter as new groups of bargoers stroll down Route 66.

Maybe someone comes in through the side door to use the microwave quietly, or maybe not. Maybe it's just me and my memory:

All those guests, friends, colleagues. The whole town, the dancing.

I see Syd, in fishnets and high boots, come to bring me snacks after surgery.

I see Faith, bad teeth and all, carrying her cleaning caddy and grinning. I hear her guffaw at my jokes. There she is, mopping, headphones in, bebopping. My mind reconstitutes her, sitting on the couch with me, kind and pensive in the small slivers of time we had between the other various frenzied aspects of life, slivers that stretched spacious enough to hold us together awhile.

There's Aiden over there in a chair, wondering why I'm so sad.

Here, alone and remembering, I forget the ways we've wronged each other, purposefully or mistakenly. I simply miss my people. At the same time, I fear to encounter them.

Maybe someday I'll be brave enough to call Faith or Syd, offer apology.

To find peace with my time spent with Aiden.

Then again, maybe not. And maybe no one cares either way.

Meantime, there are others to love.

And things I've learned. That has to serve for now.

When the rhythmic dryer stops its metallic churning, I fold the last remaining sheets.

I lock up the door and push in my chair, switch off the *Open* sign.

I'd like to make it home before Amtrak jams the tracks, spitting newcomers out into the town, whisking others away.

I know it's coming soon.

Murder City

During the day, four days a week, I go to my local community college and tutor human students in the mysteries of the English language. At night I train bots. Rather, I train a single bot, just one, working remotely to parse messages with it. To comply with our company NDA, I'll call this bot Carey. I work the late shift because Carey never sleeps, and she needs supervision even after I sign her over to the next scheduled trainer. She doesn't sleep, have a body, or get paid, but she has other human qualities: a veneer of gender, an affinity for exclamation points, and a memory far better than mine. She answers client questions by chat at a speed I'd be unable to mimic, which is why she was created. I can't tell you what our products are: suffice it to say that they're necessary.

When I mention this night job to people, most of them tell me I'm training the bot to replace me. Humans, I've learned, can be obsessively fearful of entities that pose no real threat to us, like zombies and vampires, which don't exist, or robots, which haven't actually ever done anything we haven't programmed them to do. I joke back that maybe bots *should* replace us, and not just at work. My husband and I live in one of the most violent cities in America, and we can see that it's people ourselves—not bots—causing harm: countless robberies, territorial drug disputes, police shootings. Thirteen children were gunned down, drive-by style, in north city early last month. Last week, another still-at-large suspect put a bullet through the neck of a random café patron where I sometimes sit to train Carey. And just last night, in a hold-up at a nearby south city dive bar, the drinker being robbed lit a cigarette in the middle of it, so unsurprised was he.

I tend to work from home most days. The house Tim and I rent in south St. Louis is a spacious old German-built brick fortress. Sturdy storm-proof walls. Gracefully rounded doorways. A deep, leaky basement below lacquered wood floors for Tim's band equipment. A small, muddy backyard for Bruno the Dog. But past this vague pleasantness, in the mostly empty shed at the end of this yard, the one that won't lock properly, one day appeared a spike-collared pit bull, sitting quite politely when Tim went in for a rake, awaiting an owner who'd never returned. Another day: a dirty mattress, a box of sour food, and a stash of used needles. When we put these supplies outside, the someone they belonged to broke back into the shed and shat.

Outside our house, you can walk around our neighborhood, but it isn't recommended after dark. Junkies sometimes tie off in the quiet space between our building and the look-alike next door. Sometimes they jiggle our basement doorknob. Brick is bulletproof mostly, but the swell of front-yard yelling matches carries a tension that can carve itself into a psyche, regardless. The baby-poop aroma of the corner laundromat, glass-sprayed parking lots, quasi-aggressive neighborhood beggars, and seemingly self-replicating yard litter tempt me to scout for homes farther north: not too far north, where the homes stand singed and empty and brick has been stolen to sell to shady contractors, but toward the center strip of posh parks, museums, and schools, where rent is higher.

I could add another job to afford that, right? Or pick up more hours teaching/training? Our friends ask why we don't move. If we got our debt down—most of it my student loans—we probably could, yes. Or I could prod Tim into working the extra bartending shifts he hates, or take out another loan, and go.

But in the long run, would it really solve that much? The friends we see most often—Tim's bandmates who come weekly to practice—still all seem to have second jobs to pay for their better-located houses: George a nurse, Nelson a nano-biologist,

Kyle a librarian. Linda drums for the Air Force before coming to our basement band room. Work is as automatic for us all as it is for Carey the bot. Plus, if someone else moved in here, our next-door neighbors, a poor middle-aged sibling pair, would need to find someone else to drive them for groceries. Someone else would have to duck from the nine shots fired by the guy running past the stinky laundromat. This is the thing people can't seem to get, and I wonder if robots—built by and dependent upon humans, yet harboring no illusions of contemporary lone ranger autonomy—someday might: that, despite a suspiciously lazy desire for separateness, every living and nonliving unit of existence, every person, cell, company, computer chip, or sentence, is part of a system. And any portions of the system that do not cooperate will remain fragmented, risky, like bullet spray, bright against the night.

One little spot near our house boasts a permanent drink special called the Murder City, referencing the local violence. I walk there now, still in daylight, and order it. The drink is pink and ever-so-slightly effervescent: perhaps like blood diluted, with an added splash of whimsy. I like it a lot, despite feeling guilty about liking it: complicit in a gallows humor that seems to tempt fate. I take out my laptop and double-check my bot work schedule, updated constantly as my fellow mobile trainers tackle WiFi and other logistical workflow obstacles. I'm on the schedule for tonight, but not right now, so I can relax here, maybe jot down some ideas for tutoring or a weekly to-do list for myself, gaze out the window at old brick, and contemplate the history of my new (old) city.

We didn't expect to move here: if someone had said to take an atlas and choose where we'd like to go, it wouldn't have been St. Louis. Tim and I joke that we're tracing the westward expansion in reverse, for various personal and professional reasons working backward along the Oregon and Santa Fe Trails. We foray through a grab-bag of varied environments to find the economic and creative freedoms we seek, though, and there have been many songs and stories composed about this place, the Gateway to the West; its mythology runs deep. But the city itself is now also moving in reverse: it's the fastest shrinking urban area in the country, says a city planner I know.

In St. Louis, swaths of burned-out, blighted houses exist mere blocks from the city's stateliest mansions, whose owners spend more on lawn care than their neighbors live on annually. St. Louis, a concentrated crossroads of American histories, runs a complicated tab of moral karmic cycles. It brims with tales of hardest workers: of seaboard city-slickers seeking slices of time and space for themselves, of southern slaves whose freedom took far too long to come. Of trolley lines, once serving working-class parts of town, pulled up to promise car companies new freeways and larger market shares. Of factories, locked and empty now, still looming. Of mighty rivers, irrevocably polluted. Capitalism doesn't care: it's not the concern of the wealthy what their ragged counterparts will suffer. "Lazy," "unfortunate," "ignorant," or the more accurate "they didn't learn to play the game" are the refrains I hear about the city's less fortunate, instead of "they're exhausted" or that "the game" of money itself, of competition cloaked in strategic respectability, is rigged and has been for centuries, the powerless building wealth for well-known families, whose names still grace the facades of museums and schools today. I wonder if Carey, also built for the financial benefit of others, a slave of sorts herself, knows anything of greed when she cues up responses about rising product prices. In theory, and perhaps mercifully, she knows only the patterns of words, of speech, not the larger patterns of humanity's behavior.

As I fester in all this, my phone vibrates. One of my human coworkers requests coverage from our shared group media thread for a slim ten minutes: stuck in traffic, they say. Here I am, with laptop handy, just a sip into my drink, so I volunteer. Once online, the home screen begins to boop with queries from human consumers, responding to ads from our partner companies: *Do you offer any discount? Why is the price so high?* After Carey and

I relay the basic facts we've been given, I sidestep being too direct about the decision-making process behind them: *One of our consultants can help you with this!* Then I connect them.

Sometimes the customers don't want to speak with a consultant: they want their answers right now, through chat. If they get impatient, insult Carey while thinking she's human, or get hip to the game and tell her she's just a stupid bot—*I don't deal with robots!*—the real person behind the machine of Carey, me, stops wanting to respond to them too. My fellow bot-trainers and I appreciate that Carey shields us from ill-mannered people, and we wish we could return the favor. Our community posting board brims with anecdotes about how poorly some of the human clients behave: we poke fun at them, their entitled attitudes and myriad spelling errors; we let off our own steam. But we're all in this scenario together: our company can't completely substitute me for Carey, or Carey, yet, for me. And we, all parties involved, need the clients—even the crabby ones—for our daily bread. So we'll negotiate all our needs together, in rotating four-to-five-hour shifts, twenty-four hours a day, seven days a week, every single day of the year.

I'm a person, I type, and I'm not really lying, *but I'm not the specific consultant you need. I'll put you in touch with one.*

"How's the Murder City?" asks the bartender, calling me out of my screen and back to the rough-hewn wood bar, poker machine in the corner, TV lit up with sports. The bartender's face is weathered into smile lines and brow furrows both, and he has the bearing of a man who's mastered the subtleties of when to kick foundering customers to the curb, when to tuck them into cabs, and when his guard can soften and he can enjoy a little conversation time with them.

As I hold up my half-full drink to consider, my Carey co-trainer pops into the ether of our online work system, free of her traffic jam, to finish the rest of her shift. I log out, close my screen.

"It's delicious," I say, and suck it down. "Put another on my tab."

"So what are you doing there?" He points at my computer.

"Believe it or not," I say to the man on his feet eight hours a day, pouring, cleaning, small-talking, "I was working."

Despite the relative simplicity and ease of my job compared to others I've witnessed or worked, sometimes the stresses I encounter fill up the Tetris screen of my mind. It took a lot of loan money for me to get my college degrees (multiple), to get this job (both my jobs), and some months are still quite tight: after rent and utilities are paid, the student loan bills land in the mailbox at our pretty brick home in the tough neighborhood, and my heart sinks. It grows weary of skirting failure, grows thin like a filament, or paper fragments prone to scatter. When discouragement looms, I imagine myself comfortable or I seek reprieve. I try to *fake it till I make it*: one extra cocktail, like now. Or I take myself—sometimes with Carey on the laptop, sometimes not—for a ten-dollar bowl of pho, where the owners know me as a regular and the hot soup soothes. I feel momentarily nourished as I gaze out the window and rest. I tip well on my credit card. Then I schedule my payment ahead of time from what I think will be my upcoming paycheck amount.

Other days, I drive to the nearby Big Lots, because it's the place where broke folks like me like to shop for items just a notch above immediate need. At Big Lots, it's okay to have bad neck tattoos, reek of cigarettes, eat fast food from a bag on your way in. It's okay to wear dirty flip-flops while you push the cart with the antitheft flag down each aisle, searching for things that will lift you, one object at a time, out of all this. You might be looking for a vision of orderliness, health, safety, or excitement, folded into new sheets or a home-improvement tool kit. Dreams might be concentrated in spice bottles, scented soaps, off-brand electronics. Leisure awaits in the comfy new patio chair, through the lenses of five-dollar sunglasses (prepared for the perfect sunset), or the ever-jaunty tennis "skort," ready to swim in a pinch. Research in organizational psychology has shown that even the smallest amount of decision-making power in one's life, getting to pick which color corporate-logo T-shirt to wear to work on casual Friday, can cause significant increase in satisfaction, whether the choice represents real change or not.

When should I have a consultant contact you?

For now, as I watch the bartender wipe and hang his glasses, moving back and forth behind the bar like an auto-assembly worker, I savor my position in the system, however imperfect the system itself still is.

Tomorrow I'll wake and walk the dog. Dishes, then maybe use the treadmill at the Y. I'll go to my community-college day job and tutor. My human students and I will read and write together: comprehend and express. They are the vocal versions of Carey, able to respond to me in a parallel process of pattern memorization and comprehension. They will work hard. They may groan in frustration, many just now grasping the grammar so many kids get in grade school: how to slow their sentences with stops and commas, how to pause, pivot, and capitalize, to fit the mold for conveniently common human communication. In between nursing tests, chef internships, and funeral-service vocational papers, sometimes they get to write an assignment about themselves: stories of homelessness, mothers sick or slapping, missing dads, years of food pantries, learning disabilities, drugs and premature death.

"Keep going," my fellow tutors and I say to them across our tutor tables, looking them in the eye. "Keep working. Things will get better. Doors are opening." Some days I feel I may be fibbing.

But on better days, I find our mutual hopefulness warranted. I've seen many students lean over to help one another, unrequested, despite deep differences. I've seen some develop self-love, pride, a real curiosity about the world, maybe move into more comfortable, better-paying jobs. Sometimes, when I least expect it, I get to watch my students bloom.

Like last night on my long shift: for the first time, I saw Carey stitch two standard responses together: *I have passed along your request to one of our consultants!* and *Thank you for your patience.* Maybe the bot developers lent a subtle hand in this phrase combining, or maybe Carey just watched me tag the two phrases together enough times to catch on, but either way, I gasped aloud and grinned. I posted the triumphant screenshot of successful bot-text in my coworker thread like a happy parent, and even clicked to add the hands-out emoticon for "hug," which, to me, looks more like "delight."

I decide against telling the kindly bartender more about my job. He lives in a different world anyway, and is currently busy watching another patron slur loudly into her phone: *Find me a closer Uber, Siri!*

"Has Siri even been programmed for that?" I mutter.

I side-eye the loud woman again, as her phone's preprogrammed voice echoes in apology: *Sorry, I didn't quite catch that*, and the woman grumbles: *You're worthless.*

No one besides the bartender seems to blink at the woman's anger, and I wonder: if she were yelling at another human being, rather than her pink-encased computer communicator, would someone say something? Not so long ago, it was legally and socially acceptable to abuse women and nonwhite people by the same logic that, today, we apply to edible animals and to our robots—they aren't quite "sentient" enough to respect—while simultaneously we fear their sentience ascending. What will we do, I think, if we discover, en masse, that life itself is owned, or built, or bred? Would that somehow, finally, extend our empathy?

Perhaps too much *Matrix*/Catholic school/army hierarchy, or *Ancient Aliens* for me. Either way, I tell the bartender I'll pay. I pack my bag up, leave a tip, and smile goodbye. I walk past the still griping, Uber-awaiting drunk woman and out into the neighborhood.

Past the fast-food drive-thru, frying factory-farmed livestock into burgers for growing teens.

Up the hill where I imagine I can glimpse, through the smog, the church spires ascending from the wealthier center strip of the city.

Past the new tech hub with the train stop and trendy restaurants.

Past the used auto lots, selling second-, third-, and fourth-hand cars, "freeway ready."

Over the cracked and crumbling streets, I backtrack, musing on all us in-betweeners, existing somewhere near self-made and created, natured and nurtured, in whom, against all odds, I can still sense form and dream knit together.

Here is our block, where, behind rear alley dumpsters, people in trouble slump. Where, streetside, other versions of themselves pass out rehab pamphlets.

Here is our historic rental home: a structure for life, semi-protected, to stay that way another day.

See the sturdy stone steps. Locked door. Cozy fireplace.

The big damp basement where Tim can host weekly band practice.

Where I can sip soup.

Carey can eat electricity.

Bruno the Dog can scour the yard for snacks.

Where, from one corner of the living room window, past the nearby park's sandy baseball field, old brick buildings still rise, somehow, skyward.

Hope for Sale

I work the online graveyard shift typically, so I'm sleepy in the morning as I head up the I-55 from St. Louis toward the funeral directors conference in Collinsville, Illinois. I know I need to pay close attention, because Collinsville, my friend Ron said, is a tiny town: the turnoff passes in a blip.

A giant flat-topped hill rises to view.

"Cahokia!" I murmur.

I've only seen them in photos before, these plateaus made by Cahokia's ancient mound builders, and this, by far the largest, is far larger in actuality.

I make a note to call my friend Kate as I pass; we've contemplated running a 5K event here in November.

Meantime, I catch sight of the Collinsville sign and pull off the highway into a tiny business park, where remnants of a 1970s manufacturing development still sit half-empty in the sun.

Square brown office buildings crumble into weedy parking lots.

A giant family-style restaurant waits, empty, for a lunch crowd that may or may not ever appear.

And at the end of that road: the smallest convention center I've ever seen. It's so cute!

I lap it once to make sure I'm at the right entrance, and I am, because there's only one. A little stream of suited-up Baby Boomers trickles toward the front door, briefcases and poster rolls in hand. A sign near the door, in the shadows, reads something about "Mortuary," and standing next to that is the tall, straight-backed man with glasses I'm seeking: my contact.

"Ron," in my clever obfuscation to protect his reputation, is short for "Charon," the mythical Greek ferryman of the River Styx, charged with transporting the souls of recent deceased into the afterworld. I thought this was fitting, since Ron's a funeral director. He's a regular patron at the bar where my husband works, where he's quietly regaled me, Tim, Kate, and anyone else within earshot with strange tales of the mortuary arts. He's proud of his work but ashamed of his industry.

"It's corrupt," he says.

Here's what I know so far:

There's a lot of segregation.

Christian services are the default, and sometimes hard to get the staff to deviate from.

Pricing is set in such a way as to encourage bigger package purchases, often more than families need or can afford.

Respect for the dead is . . . variable.

Ron's job and his daily life are tightly bound. He lives above one funeral parlor in St. Louis and drives his predictably brown-black company car across state lines each day to operate another location in Illinois. He spends four nights a week, sometimes more, on-call to pick up corpses, then manages sad and mad grieving families after that.

"Tim's told me a lot about you," I remember Ron saying at our first shared meal. "And I see Tim a lot." Ron had smiled, saluting Tim with his beer.

I laughed. "Oh, I think you're making an alcoholic's joke."

"Oh, it's no joke," Ron said, still smiling. Then he told me funeral directors, as an occupational group, suffer from higher-than-average rates of addiction.

"Suicide is also a popular choice," he said, citing a recently departed member of his company. But, he informed me, it's the behavior of living people, not the dead, that depresses him. Ron

Hope for Sale—185

described a family, from the forefront of his mind, who insisted that their son, gay and an AIDS victim, be memorialized in an evangelical Christian funeral service.

"The preacher demanded the congregation repent right then and there, so they wouldn't go to hell like the dead boy. He came banging down the aisle, hitting the pews with his Bible. So we had another service for his friends, later on," Ron said, "a drag show. People dressed up, karaoked . . . *celebrated*! It was the kind of remembrance the departed would have actually wanted."

But back to the convention.

What have I gotten myself into? I wonder as I join Ron near the door. This is serious stuff, and I'm mainly here out of morbid curiosity, to eavesdrop.

About what? I already know about life and death, having friends in both categories. I myself plan to bumble along as pleasantly as possible from now until I die: No. Big. Deal.

So maybe, I realize, what I want to know is why some people obsess about what happens after.

Every pamphlet I've just been handed as we're checking in contains clever cursive marketing: elegies made elegant, dignified, sometimes even almost cheerful or ecstatic.

They confuse me, the options for urns:

Rhapsody (a rather dour marble box).

Majestic (a deer head with antlers? I think).

And Serenity (of course, an angel, but oddly more orgasmic in expression than really restful).

I flip open the food options for receptions. The Tribute Appetizer Special looks fine but also easily compiled from Kroger freezer and snack aisles, including Applewood Chicken Bites, Sweet & Sour Meatballs, and a Cheese Sampler With Crackers: $695 serves twenty-five.

As I wait for Ron to laugh with me about the overpriced concoctions I'm pointing to, I realize I'm hungry. I usually sleep through breakfast hours, but here I am, wide awake. Past his rather subdued smile, I see a buffet set out for us attendees, a draping of grapes and sliced fruit, bagels, little cheeses like the ones from the Tribute menu. So I sidle toward it, taking Ron too.

"If anyone asks, you're an intern," he says, because he's gotten my ticket on the company dime.

"You don't want to say we met at a bar?" I joke, but only half-jokingly, as I'm a bad liar. "Can't we just say I'm *thinking* about mortuary school?"

But just then we're descended upon by a crew of suit-clad, suit-skirted, and suitcase-clutching funerary professionals. They all smile maniacally.

The blond man with the whitest teeth grins. "Good morning! Who's this?"

"She's a prospective intern," Ron replies.

We shake hands.

Toothy asks me what draws me to the field, how I'm liking my coursework so far. Since I know very few technical details about mortuary science, I swallow hard and tell him that embalming has me scared. I remember what Ron's told me about what keeps him working in the field, and I recite it: "I like helping families during their time of need, though. It will make it all worthwhile."

Everyone hums in agreement, then we all pile up little plates of fruit. We drain coffee from giant urns, then head together down the hall. I'm thankful that Ron and I don't see any open seats too near his coworkers: I want to be able to ask him honest questions without having to fake my allegiance to certain practices I find, privately, obsolete.

Like embalming.

Or even burial altogether.

"Soylent green is people," I murmur mentally in singsong, and why not? We have unsustainable farming practices on this planet: we'll need more food soon anyway. Suddenly starving, I stab a sausage and, even though I'm not seated yet, stick it in my mouth.

When we do sit, I survey the high-ceilinged hall around me. It's all bland beige walls, with a mottled mauve-green vomit-looking carpet threatening to float up and envelop my shoes. The room is a sea of white-on-black: mostly black-clothed Caucasians shaking hands and sitting down. Per Ron, "The National Funeral Directors Association convention is 'more white' and the National Funeral Directors & Morticians Association convention represents mainly African American directors and embalmers."

We must be at the white one.

The room is also about 70–80 percent male, old guys who have the seniority to take time off for conventions. The aging population of these directors is what is, finally, opening the death care industry, as a whole, to more women and minorities, Ron says. In fact, according to a recent poll by the National Funeral Directors Association, more than 60 percent of recent funeral service graduates are women.

The fact that I am obviously younger than most people in the room, at thirty-eight, may be what's attracting some curious glances, though. Ron's actually younger, at thirty-four, but I always think of him as closer to forty, partially due to his hairline and partially to his calm composure. I've never seen him not in a suit, never heard him yell/guffaw and/or weep, and I've never known him *not* to wait a few moments before thoughtfully answering a question, any question actually, aiming for near-perfect precision.

A rural West Virginia boy, he's grown far from his roots. He left his holy-roller church ("tongues, snakes") when none of his fellow congregants could answer queries he offered about why they followed *some* biblical tenets to the letter, but some others not at all. He'd worked as a middle-school social studies teacher until he needed to make more money, then added a night job as a body transporter. He learned how much more money funeral directors made than teachers (almost twice as much), but he didn't decide to entirely change careers until he was asked to help wire an arm back onto a motorcycle victim he was transporting. Reattaching the errant limb with the embalmer, stomach turning, Ron realized he was, in fact, capable of handling the dead. And maybe, in that field, he could make "a difference" as he had teaching, but also a livable paycheck.

"When," I ask, wide-eyed at the slides of cadavers cued up onto the 120-inch screen before us, "did you get to the point that your stomach stopped turning?"

"It never has," he says.

The first presentation of the day, full of graphic anatomical slides, is an overview of the mortuary "arts" by an ardent advocate for "traditional" body restoration. He looks a little like Bela Lugosi's Dracula, pale face starkly contrasting his slicked-back black hair and suit. He tells us the story of President Lincoln, himself an early embalming experiment. For weeks after his assassination, Lincoln's body apparently was paraded throughout America, giving the post-Civil War citizenry some comfort as they moved into the many unknowns of Reconstruction. I decide, as I listen, to call our speaker Vlad, after the medieval Romanian warlord Vlad the Impaler, who many say Dracula was modeled on.

Vlad cites John Jacob Astor, pulled up dripping from the *Titanic*, iced down to preserve him for a proper patch-up and an ensuing elite New York society funeral. He ponders John F. Kennedy, whose wife Jackie must have read Jessica Mitford's industry-skewering *The American Way of Death* prior to his passing, as she insisted on a closed-casket procession, depriving his mourners of one last presidential viewing.

Then Vlad brings himself to tears describing the importance of a properly embalmed body to the mourning and recovery process: so families can see and comprehend that their loved one is actually dead.

"Some people say the viewing isn't important, that cremation or a ceremony of remembrance should be enough—" Vlad points to the crowd "—but I've seen mothers waiting by the phone in *diapers* for their unrecovered sons to come back from wars. There are still people that rehang fresh 'Missing' posters every week in the subway stations near Ground Zero, thinking their loved ones, lost on 9/11, are still alive someplace in New York."

I lean over to Ron. "Is he exaggerating?" I whisper.

"I've had a mother calling my funeral home for months," he whispers back, "telling me we're part of a conspiracy that's captured and hidden her son from her, because all we could recover from a fire was his skeleton, which was not recognizable as him."

I put down my grapes and give up on breakfast.

Vlad's conception of funerary (and embalming) work as a kind of spiritual or social vocation, I realize, serves as the segue into the next presentation: a deep dive into the gritty details of manipulating the dead back into looking alive-ish, the component of this work many people find so disturbing. Suddenly the slides on the enormous screen include: the severely bloated face of a corpse gone swollen, an emaciated corpse face sunk flat, and a face unrecognizable as such, having been blown apart by gunshot and nearly inside-out.

Death care: so much about resetting, it seems, whether a physical body or a more elusive sense of security.

I drink my dehydrating cups of coffee while I learn about how embalming preserves and disinfects, keeps destructive bacteria from being able to attach to, or grow within, dead skin cells.

If a body looks too dried out by this process, one can add a clever chemical humectant to the arterial mixture to moisten.

You can inject a gel tissue-builder into sickly-thin corpse skin to plump it, and air-brush over jaundice.

If a corpse is bloated, like our friend onscreen, just make a slit or two, tip the body up at an angle, and drain the excess fluids out. Then you can push the tongue back into the mouth where it belongs, close the eyes into peacefulness.

Faces seem, then, to be pleasantly sleeping. I have to admit, despite my flopping stomach and general incomprehension, the transformations impress.

Maybe that's why, I think, flipping the price pamphlet open again, the cost of reconstruction is so high: a hairdo for locks soon to be submerged in earth runs $120, more than double what I pay for my own trims, and makeup is a neat $95.

Ron explains, when I question this, that industry prices reflect required training: typically an associate's or bachelor's, an up-to-two-year internship or residency, multiple national and state board exams, and then work as a director/embalmer for some years before admission into one of the few restoration-specific training programs.

The face and hands are the most important parts, he points out, as all other landscapes of a body can be covered up in clothing. Thus it is that the gunshot victim, in cases where religion demands an open casket, must be carefully reverse-engineered: The separation lines of the skull where it cracked outward must be followed, folded, and pressed back into position. The cranial cavity will be stuffed with cotton to prevent its collapse, and then it will be sutured securely with metal wire. The most important portion of the face to preserve, furthermore, is the right side, because that side will face viewers, and most caskets are hinged so as to preserve this orientation.

"Why is that?" I ask, and Ron whispers that people think Jesus will arrive again from the East. So you want to be facing the right direction, on Judgment Day, to meet him.

"I've accidentally ordered some left-opening caskets I've had to return in a hurry. With my luck, Jesus actually *will* show up and one of my clients will stand up facing the wrong way."

I find this funny.

"But what if you're not Christian?"

The industry, he says, is slowly coming around to a less Bible-based monopoly, but the right-facing coffin is still, currently, standard.

Funeral companies don't know, Ron says, that when they hire him, his agenda is progressive: to include more people in an ability to mourn well, to abolish the bigotry and decrease the pervasive discrimination he sees in hiring and service practices.

"You don't have to believe what they believe," he says of the conservative corporate entity he currently works for—one of the biggest in the nation, acquiring smaller funeral parlors almost weekly, "You just have to *act* like you do, long enough to get your foot in the door. Show up at church once in a while, do your community service requirement—walk some dogs at the local pet shelter—then you can sneak in some people of color. Put some vegan options on the menu for memorials. Offer cheaper caskets and cremation packages, hire some preachers that aren't exclusively Baptist."

On a break between panels, while Ron is off networking, I decide to detour to the giant sloping mounds of earth I passed that morning. Sun will do me good, I think, after the morgue-like convention center A/C. I text Kate and tell her I'm headed to our future racing site: November's 5K Sun Run. Running is religion for Kate, who's had a tough few years of divorce and relocation from out of state, and though I don't run that much, this location is interesting: a state park where, centuries before us, other people lived, died, and were buried. The running path winds around the mounds, and I wonder if we'll feel like we're running backward through time.

Cahokia: mysterious cluster of about a hundred ancient, flat-topped, human-hewn hills. Some of the first high-rises, I think, as I drive a meandering off-highway road through farm prairie, tractor repair shops, and feed stores to the state park's shiny visitor center. Inside I find a few bored docents, of about the same age as my last event's attendees, ready with stacks of their own brochures.

On the entry foyer wall hangs a giant map of other primordial sites, what seem like hundreds more of them: cities whose influential eras and inhabitants have passed, like this one and like we will too, into dust.

Stretching far across a plain, these particular mounds had multiple functions. Some supported various facets of living. Some, like Mound 72, it's believed, were made for burial. In fact,

Mound 72 was, I guess, made for mass burial: more than 270 bodies tucked away together, a few elites centered in the middle, bathed in twenty thousand river-shell beads and hundreds of regional arrowheads.

I step outside and take a wandering route through golden grasses, slowly passing mound after mound. I'm not moving at contemporary speed anymore—in my car, or on a train or plane—I'm just walking, seeing this land as the ancients likely did. It's quiet but for the whisper of grass, and I like it.

Sweat beads on my forehead as I make my way to the largest, Monk's Mound, about a hundred feet tall and a thousand feet wide: like if you stacked ten African elephants on top of each other, and then stretched twelve and a half giant female blue whales tip to tail.

Ascending the enormous stairway up it, my thighs strain and my butt burns. When I arrive, I recall that I have lungs.

As I straighten to catch my breath, I catch sight of the vast valley below: the deceptively slow-seeming soft brown river, and also industry rising, slate gray and rugged, the sharp modern buildings making the new Mississippi reality nearby.

Like the river over there, my life in Missouri seems to seep along slowly through egregiously long and lingering winters, sun-soaked and perpetually mosquito-bitten summers. But like the river's undertow, or a sudden summer lightning storm, time, I know, can jolt people from our autopilot in thunderclap or gun flash before we understand what's gone. I gaze over the hazy humid sky, only half blue, and wonder if I'll realize when I've run out of time. Did the people before?

I look at my watch: I must return.

Back at the convention center, I find the next three panels fascinating.

One is about helping children to participate in memorials, with the general takeaway that "children who don't grieve properly never recover emotionally."

One's about field-specific legal concerns: don't fire a funeral director if they change genders, lest you get sued.

The last is a series of pro tips for marketing to seniors: Not so much on Facebook. They still like newspapers!

As I listen to each speaker stress the crucial social value of the service they provide ("It can take a grieving person six-plus years to recover from losing a parent, yet most community support dries up after one!"), I run my finger down the extra "add-ons" column of a pamphlet.

This column seems to give surviving relatives a way to have one last little impact, and a sense of creative control about how they mourn: casket medallions, sign-in books, prayer cards, a dove release, a balloon release, a lifelike portrait etched into glass, a flag case. You may not be able to make Mom alive again, or erase the conflicts you had before her passing, but you can pick and choose her memorial trinkets: how to represent her now. It's satisfying, I suppose, like any shopping: a decision-making process that provides a sense of accomplishment, something to *do* in the face of loss.

Or at least distraction.

I find myself thinking about how many bad poems I've written during moments of duress. And they did help.

When these panels peter out, I can hear my belly, mostly breakfast-deprived, begging for sustenance. So Ron and I drive to Ruby Tuesday.

As I slice into my salmon, steaming pink and salty, I think of how good the normally mediocre fast-casual chain food tastes: even buttered broccoli brims with an urgent feeling of nourishment, of satiation and survival, and the knot in my stomach loosens. I'm alive! I gaze past the traffic, sun glinting on so many metal car doors, past field grass blanketing the hill back toward our conference, one jarring reality sliding seamlessly into another like fish flesh into my mouth.

"Listen," I say, "this job seems incredibly difficult, in a myriad of ways." I relate what I've noticed: the *constant* reminder of mortality, the weird twilight hours on call, the emotional explosiveness that can burst forth from mourning humans.

Plus, corpses.

"What part is hardest for you?" I inquire.

Ron, a person I usually encounter lightening his mood with lager, takes a draw from his chaste lunchtime lemonade.

"I hate how hard it is to keep relationships," he says seriously.

"You mean, romantic, or just in general?"

"Both."

He clarifies that death care professionals can have a hard time relating to friends and partners (or anyone) about their daily experience.

"I can see that," I say.

"Couples grow apart. You're constantly half available, always interrupting important conversations to step out and take a call, leaving for hours three or four nights a week, at three or four a.m. It's hard to develop trust in a relationship when you're always on the phone, always out late, cancelling plans last minute."

He describes being halfway through preparing his grandpa's body for his funeral when the coroner dropped off a newly deceased young woman, pregnant with twins. She'd thrown herself from a local bridge, hitting several beams on her way to the water. Her grieving husband wished the twins buried not only with her but inside her, so Ron spent that night reconstructing an artificial womb and stitching the prematurely separated entities all back together for the horrified family. Then, and only then, he turned his attention back to his own grandpa.

"How do you talk about that over dinner?" he asks.

As we drive back down our little blacktop strip toward the conference, I realize why Ron's so thin: you lose not just one appetite but several.

And meanwhile you still have to hustle: we beeline to the showroom, then Ron peels off to hunt down someone he calls "the big boss," who had lunch, in his absence, with a competitor for a coming promotion. This competitor has apparently been shifting money from their funeral home to cover up losses at their cemetery, and Ron calls foul.

I'm left, then, to wander aisles of urns, sympathy tokens, and shiny hearses in solitude.

I start to think about the kinds of things that make meaning at a memorial: how people attempt to stitch material trappings of living to a person's emotional life history, or at least their perceived identity.

As I wander through these trappings—pamphlets, prayer cards, flower arrangements—I think of services I've been to personally, recalling one I walked out of, my dear dead friend Dante's, when his family, kind but Catholic to a fault, decided a Mass, complete with communion, was appropriate for their atheist son.

My eyes pop at the cost of the caskets. A gold-handled cherrywood Presidential would go for a whopping ten grand, but even the Medium Density Fiberboard with printed-on woodgrain finish (not present in the showroom, only listed) is still $450: half my rent for a month.

I skirt Toothy, from Ron's company, who drifts toward me from the corner and who I fear will ask me more questions about mortuary school, and then find myself lost, swirling alone in a sea of afterlife accessories, wondering how to find the door.

Back at home later, my phone vibrates.

"Wanna take a walk?"

It's Kate, texting back about our new favorite place: a local park. We have a habit, or at least the infancy of a habit, of walking through Tower Grove in the evening and catching up along the pawpaw grove, rumored to produce a banana-like fruit that Kate, sometime, wants to cook with.

And Kate can't stop cooking, she says: it calms her.

In addition to the recent divorce and relocation roller-coaster, Kate also deals with bipolar disorder, and I've only known her this way: shifting moods and energy levels.

Her stringent excellence as a furniture designer, a sneaky sense of black humor, and a ready compulsion to exercise/cook/build shit all day long help her to outsmart her anxious mind. While I sleep late after night shifts, she traverses miles and miles each day before her day job, undertaking grueling training regimens for various seasonal marathons. Her hair falls over one eye, partially concealing her feelings, while her thin fingers itch to make raw matter into more. She also loves to help people: coming to clap, dance, overtip, and otherwise generally support the local open mic nights, escaping her mania in music.

Sometimes, after the mania passes and a predictable pessimism replaces it, she has to leave her knives with a neighbor to keep herself safe.

I text Kate back from my slightly unstable stance in my own kitchen, trying to juggle the heat-involved construction of dinner, more dead flesh (this time pork) turned into tasty nutrition.

"Yeah, let's walk!"

Perhaps I'll tell her, when we meet up then, of my currently creeping misgivings: that, gazing down earlier at the range of flat-topped might-be-burial mounds, maybe galloping together in a great enthusiastic group for a fun race across it might be like trampling a contemporary cemetery. Especially given the conditions of conquered native people in this country now, Kate, always kind, will feel bad when I mention it like this. But I should: perhaps, if the dead can still sense in any vague, weird way, they'd feel sorrow at witnessing our still-active selves, potent, vibrant, capable.

Maybe Kate and I could just walk quietly to the top of that tallest mound sometime, and consider life more reverently there: see it unfolding, still, for miles.

Hope for Sale—197

About a week later, Ron and I take another trip. At his funeral home, the branch in Illinois, the cemetery is lovely, lush and rolling. It strikes me as a relaxing place to work. The breeze is soft, and sunlight filters down through well-groomed trees as we stroll together down a row.

I point at a swan. Life-sized but plastic, it's the only garish thing I see before noticing that the grave bouquets are also artificial.

"An angry daughter of a client killed our real swan with her car when she thought we weren't keeping her mother's headstone clean enough."

Amidst my exclamations, he explains: "Grief is a kind of insanity. There's no logic in it."

The behavior Ron goes on to describe—family members who scream during services, threaten to sue if postmortem makeup doesn't look the way Grandma herself would have applied it with her brush—makes me revise my moments-ago thinking that the profession is quiet and peaceful.

"Here," says Ron, stepping off the path, "you can see where the earth has sunk in a bit."

The resident under there, he says, didn't opt for an "outer burial container," required in some cemeteries so that rain-heavy earth doesn't cave in a casket over time. Made from a variety of materials, the less elaborately vault-like start at seven hundred dollars, though you could easily spend more.

"What if," I ask, "—and I know this might sound crazy—what if I *want* my body to meet with earth eventually? Maybe, you know, feed a tree or something in the future?"

Currently in America, Ron explains, "natural" burials like that, without embalming and other barriers, are rarer, though poised for a comeback though the Green Burial Movement. Quasi-hippies like myself, aiming for low impact on the planet, can even be buried in "mushroom suits" to decompose faster, or be "chemically cremated" with alkaline hydrolysis, producing no conventional carbon smoke, only an inert liquid poured safely down a drain.

"Pour me down a drain!" I cheer.

The liquid from alkaline hydrolysis is organic and beneficial to municipal water treatment facilities too, says Ron.

"A lot of people, though," he admits, ushering me into the metal embalming room, "don't want to think about Aunt Sue going to the worms, so the goal of the industry has basically become to preserve and isolate the body." Also the most expensive way to go.

"But it sounds lonely," I say.

"And," he agrees, opening a cabinet full of chemicals, "it's really just as grotesque and intrusive as the worms."

I swallow hard at some worm-shaped tubes leading to the sink from the foot-end of two metal tables, and I can't help thinking of mummies.

The removal of things that could rot.

The weird imaginary power of preservation.

"For draining?" I point to the tubes.

Not much has changed.

"A trocar and a hydro aspirator tube for cavity fluids."

I could correspondingly vacate my stomach, but I don't.

"Then," Ron goes on, "you can begin the more delicate work."

In our highly specialized American society, morticians are some of the only people tasked with this peculiar kind of labor: pumping preservatives, fastening eyes and mouths shut, stitching, clamping, and plugging potentially leaky orifices.

And they have to know their stuff: many of those chemicals lining Ron's cabinet are toxic. Some contemporary medications, when mixed with the wrong embalming formulas, can turn a corpse a gentle Smurf blue, and most embalmers keep Narcan on hand in case of accidental fentanyl exposure through a contaminated corpse.

I balk when Ron tells me of old-school pros he's known, when he first joined the industry, who worked without gloves.

"They have to wear them now," he says, leading me forward to another door.

Even in a crematorium, he goes on, there are hazards: radioactive prostate implants, after failing to cure cancer in the living, can accumulate, if unnoticed, creating an (unknown) unsafe environment.

The door swings open. I stand before the furnace, monolithic, burning quietly away. It reminds me of the pottery kiln at my high school, but of course long instead of tall and, because of this, a bit sinister.

The room is pleasantly warm, though.

"There's someone in there right now," I say.

"Yep."

Ron takes a reading from a temperature dial, writes it on a clipboard hanging nearby. Over on a tall metal workbench, he brings out a labeled box of ash.

"This is what will be left."

The box is so small.

"Are they all so small?" I say.

He tells me the amount can vary: because bone is most of the matter left over from incineration, the weight of one person's "ash" to another's has no relationship to their physical size in life.

Example: a thin man with dense bones might leave more remains behind than a heavier woman with osteoporosis.

Something occurs to me as I look at the two boxes together.

"How do you keep the ash separate?"

"Well," Ron says, "it's not an exact science."

There's a sweeping procedure now, though, performed between procedures.

People would probably get mad if they knew of this potential ashy overlap, though I can't quite say why. To me, bringing home a little of someone else with my dead loved one would comfort me: like they got to have some company, a slumber party in their urn.

But Ron knows why.

"It's the same reason," he says, "that people threaten to dig up and move their buried white grandmother if we start to inter black bodies in 'their' cemeteries." One family showed up with the original deed from the 1960s clearly stating, in bold print at the bottom, that the cemetery was "white only."

Although death is our universal equalizer, the living still love to segregate.

In the adjoining chapel it is quiet, closed off, a feeling familiar from my childhood Catholic experience of church.

There's a thick accumulation of hope, the heavy weight of wanting in the little collection of candles waiting for firelight, piano keys calm before fingertips, in the plush-piled beige carpet, ready to absorb hushed murmurs.

The room's floor-to-vaulted-ceiling windows overlook the silent pond beyond their glass.

There's the fake swan.

Up at the front of the room, after an army of gold-rimmed chairs, stands a tripod with a posterboard: a painted image of Christ, alive.

"And if the family's not Christian?" I ask. "Do you all ever serve Buddhists or Muslims, or Wiccans?"

"Then I take the poster down. I had one worker tell me he'd quit before he'd move Christ into a closet for me. 'So quit,' I told him.

"Upper management can be slow to get on board with alternative services," Ron continues, "but I have to insist. We're one of the only places in rural Illinois where Hindu families can walk with their deceased into the cremation room. For Hindu mourners, the oldest son or nearest male relative to the decedent is supposed to light the pyre. Here, they can at least push the button."

On the way back to the car, we make one last stop: a quick swing through the office, the only part of the property where we've encountered other living humans so far.

The calming green carpet is another sound-muting sponge.

The pleasant, nicely dressed "counselors" (salespeople), office managers, and other funeral directors who seem to have all arrived there smile curiously, ask me how my classes are going, and I say I still have trouble with embalming.

Ron shows me a file room full of boxes—records of long-dead clients, buried before computers became common, saved here in case the deceased's elderly spouse finally passes and now needs their partner plot. I have the same nervous reaction to the closet of boxes that I have to the idea of graveyards: stacks and stacks of people piled together, but here represented only in ink.

The adjoining room is where sales happen. I watch a well-coiffed woman work her magic, showing off options from a book. Maybe, money aside, she'd just try to make people feel better by providing completion: a satisfactory ending to whatever came before.

You can do right by your dead in the end, despite the imperfect path to get there.

◆

It's Thanksgiving now: holiday of colony, kindness, and requiem all at once.

We skipped the Cahokia 5K.

And Kate, who threw a disk in her back while training, has not been able to run, so she's especially restless. She wants to host a dinner for our friends.

She's insisted on cooking *all* of the food: "Just bring wine."

And so we do, taking our usual park route past the pawpaws, naked now, past the oak leaves inflamed against incoming winter. Brown and matted dead matter already blankets the ground, already en route to be fertilizer. On our way over, I get a message from Ron: on call for his new job, occupied and unable, currently, to join us.

I'm bummed but also relieved, as I'm struggling still to pen this article I started about his work. I think he'd like me to help him hold people accountable in his industry, and someday soon

I'll make an articulate, emotional case for change, following up the former indictments he's mentioned and seeking solutions. But I dread the more I read: about the draining of grieving people's pocketbooks, about the poisonous embalming practices and carbon-spewing cremations. The subject has become hard to think about, much less write about. And shortly after our conference, it seems, Ron was passed over for the promotion he wanted. He couldn't make any of the changes he'd hoped to, and within the same week he was fired and escorted off the premises. The employee he'd fired for telling a black funeral director her white husband couldn't "flaunt their mixed-race marriage" by bringing her lunch had, in his absence, been rehired. Officially, the reason on Ron's slip was "incompatibility with the company mission," although, his former coworkers tell him now, rumors floated that he'd gotten a DUI in the company car and had gay affairs with other staff.

"I hope they're saying it was the cute groundskeeper with the beard," joked Ron. Then he got a new job. Time would tell if it was better.

When Tim and I arrive at Kate's, rubbing our feet free of rain, we smell the spread before we see it. Vegetarian since her divorce, but an expert woodswoman deer-dresser since long before it, Kate has made meat: a whole roasted turkey and smoked cayenne pork loin. Potatoes, garlic-mashed and buttered, beckon us to the kitchen's center island. There's no formal dinner table, since her apartment is small, so we'll eat in an even more cozy family fashion—cuddled together on couches and armchairs, two of us slung aside a card table shoved against a wall. We heap the yams, jalapeno glazed, onto plates beside the microgreen bean salad. Little washes of whiskey whet our palate while we toast. Are there two different dessert choices, dairy and gluten free, just for me?

You bet there are.

As evening seeps into night, there is mirth and laughter. Everyone there, maybe ten of us or so, gets the chance to chat with everyone else. Everyone's full and it's feeling like nearly time to go when one more friend arrives, Nelson, bringing beer and his new girlfriend, who everyone can see is wasted.

She, I'll call her Drunk Girlfriend, has met Kate only once before, but decides to give her grief about a comment, meant harmlessly at that last meeting, which New Girlfriend has taken as an insult.

Kate responds by apologizing profusely.

Drunk Girlfriend is on a drunk mental loop, though, and won't let it go.

As she's led back out the door by Nelson, still complaining, Kate bursts into tears.

"You did nothing wrong," we all echo. "That [insert dirty word here] was drunk!"

We persuade her to sit and prop her feet while we clean: make her headspace hopefully clearer by tidying and Tupperwaring and scrubbing cookware.

When Kate seems calmer, we go home.

Watch TV.

Turn in early.

In the morning I hit the gym and buy some flowers. We drop them on Kate's doorstep passing north for more Thanksgiving: a little extra gratitude for her, an affirmation that she's loved.

When she texts "Thanks!" and that if we want to hang out later, she'd love to, I miss the message; second Thanksgiving dinner runs long, and I don't respond till late, en route to bed again.

Then at work the next day, I get the call that, somehow, so quickly, we've lost Kate.

It's odd, that euphemism we use to discuss death: "lost," like you could somehow simply misplace a person, set them down somewhere and forget where, and then they're gone when you remember.

Which, I guess, is what it feels like.

Kate's apartment is pretty much the way we left it on Thanksgiving, reconvening there not even a week after. The flowers we left on her porch have teleported to the table, still fresh and tall in the vase. There's a group of us there again, many of the same, but the tone has changed.

The story goes like this: two friends saw Kate's cat creep across the back lawn, crying, and when they went to take him back, they found her front door ajar. When they did, they knew something was wrong.

I sit alone later and imagine it: a hanging.

She steps off a chair over and over in my mind.

While I chastise myself for not returning her last message, she throws the rope over the back porch beam and tests it with her weight.
    Walks to the door.
    Cracks it for the cat.
    Then she comes back to the chair, climbs up, and thunders down again and again into oblivion.

There's barely time to mourn before she's gone further, back across the country with her parents in a box: cremated by the company that recently fired Ron.
    We, Kate's friends, make an impromptu memorial and watch a slide show about her. The pictures in the slideshow loop frequently, since she mostly shirked being photographed.
    Later, Tim will swear he caught a glimpse of her sitting in the corner, sketching and sticking her tongue out, while his neck hair prickled.
    The friend who made the slideshow will say that when he made it, the image of her flipping off the camera froze on his computer screen.

The day after her memorial, Tim and I lunch late. We seek solace, a reprieve from grieving, so we go for pho, hot soup that comes quick.

Tim picks up a basil leaf, presses it, and rolls it between his fingers.

"You know, we both know what it's like to want to stop existing," he says.

He's referring to an impulse I've mentioned before to him: as a teen, to set sail from my barred upstairs window onto the backyard sundial, or to down a bottle of pills after a love-fail in my twenties. He's referring to his own intermittent struggles with depression.

"But then we'd never smell fresh basil again."

He holds the crushed plant to my nose and I breathe.

It smells of spring.

The waitress fills our water glasses.

The worst horror, for me, I tell him, for I understand her drive to leave, is the chance that Kate could have changed her mind mid-fall.

Maybe she smelled remnant food from her kitchen, halfway down, and remembered the parts of living that she loved: sensory delight, or the friends and family she could share this with.

Now, of course, I have to put down my spoon to cry.

"Is she still falling, while we're out here living?" I whisper.

Another horror becomes equally hard to reconcile, one I realize later: we'd been eating, talking, and laughing our way through a second holiday dinner while she died alone in her home.

◂▬▸

It's spring again.

COVID-19 has cut swaths through communities the way I now cut through the neighborhood park.

I haven't seen much of other people lately.

Most state parks, I find when I try to return to Cahokia, are closed for quarantine; however, this one, Tower Grove, still admits visitors.

So I walk the dog here: to clear my head, to stretch our housebound muscles. We've spent a lot of time inside. A lot of time online.

I've had a lot of time to ask questions and ponder Kate's passing, while also contemplating what I've learned about "death care."

And just like those folks I heard of at Ron's convention, obsessing over their dead—waiting in diapers for the call that won't come, screaming at the mortuary hairdressers—I too have unexpectedly found myself perseverating, pestering people for more information about how Kate's death occurred, seeking salvation in some little detail or another.

I replay the days leading up to her death, imagining the scene: Thanksgiving, and what we could have done differently.

I say mean things about Drunk Girl who provoked her.

I keep my phone on, and nearby now, in case anyone calls or texts, needing anything.

I google bipolar disorder. I google what happens to the body when it hangs.

I dig.

I ask.

I seek.

What I don't do is sleep.

But here, in the park, I happen into someone on the sidewalk, an acquaintance who'd been around when Kate was found, and a tiny detail comes up in conversation.

As I walk away, I use it to sell myself some hope about what happened:

Though there had been a chair, there hadn't, after all, been a leap.

Rather, "gentle strangulation" Google tells me on my phone, is the slang term for what Kate devised to do the day after Thanksgiving: a determined person (which she always was) could lean back into a chair, tip their head aside to give a rope some purchase, then press an important major artery down slowly, cutting off blood to the brain. Gravity does the rest, and

Hope for Sale—207

the determined person loses consciousness before they start to suffocate.

Here is what I say to myself:
    Kate *did* have a choice to stand up, after all.
    Had she changed her mind, she could, still, have stood.
    And in this vision I make now, maybe she suffered less: simply eased into infinity.

I consider calling Ron to tell him I finally get it: the funerary industry isn't just selling candles and reception meatballs. It sells hope in the shape of meatballs, and that's why some people, who need desperately to make the sudden lack of life, in a life full of lengthy living, make sense, will pay so dearly for them.
    But I don't call Ron: I'm sad, and he's busy.
    As I pass the pawpaw patch in the park where Kate used to forage for fruit, I wonder if that's where the park people will plant Kate's tree. A group of us took up a collection for it, this tribute, this designated place to pause time.

Ron's busy for the same reason the park workers can't plant Kate's tribute tree till later: it's risky out here. All nonessential workers in the United States have been furloughed, or told to work from home, while Ron, an essential "last responder," is slammed, fighting for face masks while his employees brace for waves of coronavirus victims already piling high, literally, grotesquely, in bigger cities. On TV we see bulldozers clear pits for mass burial. Tim and I, along with most of our acquaintances, stay home.
    We worry and wait for whatever is going to happen to happen.
    The only thing to do, away from our computer screens, is hope, eat, and walk this dog in this park.

As I turn and head onward, I find myself wondering.
    If we lived in a world less obsessed with attaining perfection, or at least performing it, would Kate, always anxious, have felt more comfortable existing here?

My dead friend Dante, who'd escah-payed from his short life decades ago now, refused to play the game, to run the human race, or if you're tireder, the "treadmill," and who could blame him? Kate had actually tried, and still always felt she fell short.

If human communities put the kind of energy that we put into grooming and mourning our dead into people still living on the brink of death, could this life, finally, be less abrasive? Could we learn to live in peace, not just come to rest at its end?

But it seems we can't stop trying to know ourselves through our vanishings.

I wish I, this wannabe reporter failing her way into elegy, could have something more meaningful to say about the inevitable nature of cessation now, and the industry built to soothe people into it.

I don't yet. So in lieu of better options, I'll walk these laps in the park and await word of Kate's tribute tree.

About a way to remember one person.

About when it's safe to plant again.

Epilogue   Drive (IV)

"None of these guys are in there for the long haul," said a friend, encouraging me not to fear an unusual group I'd agreed to lead. "It's jail, not prison. Petty crimes. Or they're waiting to transfer."

Tucked behind an old lumber mill, temporary home to roughly five hundred, the Coconino County Jail, to me, felt like a fortress. I'd been teaching, for some years now, at the local college, and I liked it: I could sleep in, make my schedule, and carve out free time for travel over breaks. More important, teaching was helping me by helping me to (or at least providing hope that I might) help others. It was good for me to put myself aside to try to guide, encourage, and remind my students that reality is semi-malleable, and in turn my students reminded me: the more you know, the more it's possible to know. It's far from a perfect system we inhabit here, but learning is a starting point to change.

However, this was a whole different level of faith in that premise.

Inside the jail, past the fingerprinting station where I'd dipped and rolled each finger the other day, one heavy steel door after another tumblered open, then shut and locked behind me.

My pulse was racing again.

"The best way to find yourself is to lose yourself in service," I said, to self-soothe, following Gandhi's great philosophy down the hall behind a guard. The hall spit us out into a room, barred and full of orange-clad men bigger than me, older than me, and staring at me expectantly.

Then we had to start the workshop, the supervising officer and I. He watched while I talked. At first my voice wavered. The walls, tall and concrete, seemed to suck the sound of my speaking away. And what if I got stuck there? If the guards got a memo from the fingerprinters up front that I'd gone AWOL years back, and they misplaced the discharge papers, or the locking system glitched, and there I'd remain, alone and female in front of the room, trying to say something meaningful about literature.

But after some minutes, time began to ease us together. The men were quite polite: all of them, every race and phase of dental disrepair represented, were holding pencils, waiting to write. Most, I gathered, were here for drugs, bench warrants, or DUIs. I asked the men what they liked to think about. To read. To watch. What they loved and feared. I gave them prompts to start stories, fashion fictions.

As they began to write, I found I could breathe again: nothing so bad in this block.

At the end of the hour, when the sound of scribbling ceased, they shared their work: some sci-fi, some adventure, many family-themed. They wrote about things they missed or had seen, things they wished to witness or wished their characters did differently.

Then we discussed how to imagine those shifts.

Every once in awhile a prisoner stood, left his table, and climbed the metal stairs to the second floor of open cells. Just out of sight but un-doored, they peed, and the urine streams echoed out loudly. But beyond that odd interruption, it didn't feel like a jail anymore, just a room with people talking about things that interested them, in bodies that still lived and, sometimes, needed emptying.

My arm motioned out in an arc over the whiteboard. Multicolored markers reinforced this action.

"As characters move over obstacles," I said, "they make choices, have chances to change."

We agreed how it's possible to write the endings of our stories far away from where they started, characters baby-stepping toward better.

"Progress," one man offered, as the officer behind me stood up, "is a process."

And we nodded.

Then the pencils were collected, the men were lined up toward the labyrinth, and I was marched, closely chaperoned, in the other direction back past the locking doors to the lobby.

In the lobby was a bathroom, and my bladder reminded me that I had indeed been nervous.

There, in the privacy of a gray metal stall, I sat far too long staring at the toilet paper roll.

What a beautiful invention.

What a safe and silent stall.

Nobody came to knock, to demand that I move.

Eventually I unlatched the metal door, washed my hands, and stepped out into the day, leaving the little electric light on behind.

Acknowledgments

Thanks beyond measure to the Crux series editors and the University of Georgia Press for finding value in this work.

An also enormous thank-you to the writing programs at Washington University, Northern Arizona University, and Prescott College, especially to Melanie Bishop, Nicole Walker, Kathleen Finneran, Kenny Cook, and Edward McPherson, whose mentorship meant permission for me to keep writing, despite worldly pressures to become a paralegal or some other such practical professional.

I have deepest gratitude for Adam and Diane Stafford, Anna Vlahiotis, Ashley Drake, Ben Craigie, Ben McClendon, Brandon Lee, Christian Wight, Dillon Edlund, Elizabeth Brown, Erin Wahl, Gabe Montesanti, Gabe Temme, Grace Vajda, Gwen Niekamp, Jawziya Zaman, Jill Fragale, Jonny Escalante, Katie Rice-Guter, Kerri Quinn, Khara House, Libby Copa, Lindsay Dragan, Lindsay Kelsey, Lisa McCulloch, Louie Herron, Molly Wood, Monica Maggio, Nick Sommerhiser, Rachel Koch, Rebecca Mancuso, Robert Keegan, "Ron," Ryan Marr, Sanna Cheng, Shelley Staples, Sonni Pinto, Sylvia Sukop, and Yogendra Singh. Your own works have impressed and inspired me so much throughout the years.

Without the Millay Arts Foundation, the Frederick and Francis Sommer Foundation, the Arizona Commission on the Arts, and the Paragraph, NY writing room, which have all afforded me time and space I needed for this book, it might not have been finished at all. Readers, please consider supporting these amazing organizations.

I humbly acknowledge and honor the hardworking literary journals that saw fit to print some version of these essays previously, and whose ongoing endeavors continue to be essential to the life of literature in these times: *Huffpost, New England Review, Missouri Review, North American Review, Literary Hub, Witness, Hayden's Ferry Review, COMP,* and *Alligator Juniper.*

Enormous thanks to my Tim and to our families, so generous with love and support, and to all other writers whose efforts have also changed the landscape of my heart for the better.

Lastly, I offer a belated but important "I owe you" to Mrs. Rose Arnold, my grade-school English teacher, who opened this challenging, mysterious, and illuminating path for me, and likely for many others too, so many years ago.

About the Author

Lydia Paar is the winner of the 2020 Terry Tempest Williams Prize in Nonfiction. Her work has been noted in 2022's *Best American Essays* and published in leading literary journals. She lives in Tucson, Arizona, where she teaches at the University of Arizona.